Second Row
Piano
Side

200 .4092 PIE
Pierce, Chonda.
Second row, piano side

Nov-15-2000

D1043853

1201 9100 131 483 0

Second Row
Piano
Side

With humor, heartache, and hope,
Chonda Pierce tells her story

CHONDA PIERCE

BROWNSBURG PUBLIC LIBRARY
450 South Jefferson Street
Brownsburg, IN 46112

Beacon Hill Press of Kansas City
Kansas City, Missouri

Copyright 1996
by Beacon Hill Press of Kansas City

ISBN 083-411-5891

Printed in the
United States of America

Cover Design: Mike Walsh
Cover Photo: Michael Allen

All Scripture quotations not otherwise designated are from the *Holy Bible, New International Version*® (NIV®). Copyright © 1973, 1978, 1984 by International Bible Society. Used by permission of Zondervan Publishing House. All rights reserved.

Permission to quote from the following additional copyrighted version of the Bible is acknowledged with appreciation:

The Living Bible (TLB), © 1971. Used by permission of Tyndale House Publishers, Inc., Wheaton, IL 60189. All rights reserved.

Scripture quotation marked KJV is from the King James Version.

Library of Congress Cataloging-in-Publication Data
Pierce, Chonda.
     Second row, piano side: with humor, heartache, and hope: Chonda Pierce
tells her story / Chonda Pierce.
       p.   cm.
    ISBN 0-8341-1589-1
    1. Pierce, Chonda.   2. Christian biography—United States.
3. Humorists, American—Biography.   4. Wit and humor—Religious
aspects—Christianity.   5. Country music.   I. Title.
BR1725.P514A3   1996
280'.4'092—dc20
[B]
                                        96-11035
                                           CIP

10   9   8   7   6   5   4   3

To Mother

Contents

How Firm a Foundation

How firm a foundation, ye saints of the Lord,
Is laid for your faith in His excellent Word!
What more can He say than to you He hath said,
To you who for refuge to Jesus have fled?

"Fear not; I am with thee. O be not dismayed,
For I am thy God, I will still give thee aid.
I'll strengthen thee, help thee, and cause thee to stand,
Upheld by My gracious, omnipotent hand."

—John Rippon's *Selection of Hymns,* 1787

Foreword

While sitting in the auditorium of the Grand Ole Opry in Nashville one Saturday night while Little Jimmy Dickens was singing, I leaned over to a friend and asked, "You know how far it is from this seat to that stage?"

He said, "Not really."

"A lifetime," I said.

You know how far it is from the "second row, piano side" to the Grand Ole Opry? In Chonda Pierce's case, not quite a lifetime. (Well at least three-fourths of a lifetime—she's a lot older than she looks.)

Several years ago a friend of mine handed me a tape. I get handed a lot of tapes. I listen to them all—sometimes for not more than a few seconds, but at least I listen. My friend Norman Holland said, "Her name is Chonda Pierce, and she's real funny." I've heard that a lot too. But Norman is one of the goofiest people I know, and I figured he'd know funny when he heard funny.

He was right: Chonda Pierce *is* funny. Her hair is blond, Clairol No. 501 Natural Bleached Blond. Her voice is natural—it's high, squeaky, and at times *very loud,* but I guarantee you couldn't turn on the radio and hear that voice and have any doubt about who it was. And her mouth is never at a loss for words.

When I first met Chonda I was very impressed. She has a wonderful husband and two beautiful children. If you really count Zach the way he really should be counted, they have two and a half kids, so their quiver is full.

Chonda joined me on my "Comic Belief" tour. She hit the stage that first night, and I knew I'd found a star. She opened her mouth—something similar to a piece of chalk crossing a chalkboard at an angle not meant by the chalk manufacturers—filled the air, and traveled through the microphone, out the speakers, and to the awaiting ears of the people, old and young alike, who fill the auditoriums across the great land. Everyone sat up. Children quit squirming. Old men adjusted their hearing aids. Mothers relaxed their shoulders as they began to laugh. And laugh they did!

After those early concerts I noticed that Chonda was the same onstage as she was off. She never changed. What you saw is what you got. In fact, I had to teach her one day what an "inside voice" was. There's a voice we use for the stage, a voice we use when projecting to thousands of people from a platform, and there's a voice we use while cramped in a bus traveling to the next concert. But every now and then, as hard as she tries, Chonda gets excited about something and . . . ouch . . . screech . . . stop . . . *here comes her outside voice.*

Probably the most powerful thing I've ever seen happen on a concert stage was watching Chonda "make the turn." She would have those audiences laughing about her childhood, and the next thing you knew she was giving her testimony. You never saw it coming. While she had your mouth open in laughter, she reached down and touched your heart. You know you can't laugh with your arms folded. And when your arms come down, so do the defenses. And when they laugh, you know they're listening.

Chonda never gives them time to quit listening. From her stories of laughter to her stories of tears, Chonda communicates the same silver thread from beginning to end. A thread of hope. A thread that leads through laughter, disappointment, loss, broken promises—and has finally led Chonda back to a place of hope again.

Don't start this story without plans to finish. Follow the thread. It will take you to places you've been and places you pray you'll never go.

Chonda, I'm proud of you.

But remember—use your "inside voice."

—Mark Lowry
Word Recording Artist

Backstage at the Grand Ole Opry

*O*CTOBER *28, 1994. Backstage was a hubbub of activity and excitement. People were shaking each other's hands and slapping each other on the back. Lots of stories were being told that began with "Why, I remember when . . ." I saw one gray-haired man standing in the hallway and tuning his banjo. There were lots of cowboy hats. Groups of two or three would suddenly freeze, and flashbulbs would wash the whole room.*

I was told it was like this every Friday night—and I was supposed to go onstage at 7:09 P.M.—the same stage on which the likes of Roy Acuff, Barbara Mandrell, Hank Williams, Garth Brooks, Ricky Skaggs, and Cousin Minnie Pearl had performed.

A young man with a pad and pen asked me a couple of questions and wrote down a few things on a note card. He said it was for Little Jimmy Dickens, who would be introducing me tonight. A lady with a big comb made some adjustments to my hair. Another lady put some powder on my nose. They seemed a bit embarrassed when they asked, "Now, who are you anyway?"

A friend who had come along with me had to raise her voice slightly in order for me to hear her say, "I like the red dress, but wear the blue one instead!"

A man with a headset and a folded sheet of paper that he kept opening and reading, anxiously checked his watch, then came and led me and my freshly powdered nose away. I passed my husband, who was in the green room. He didn't look well.

I, too, was a bit embarrassed when I had to ask, "Now, who is Little Jimmy Dickens?" Without answering, the stage manager led me through a series of doors and to the shadowy backstage area. We stopped just at the edge of the arc of light. He pointed to a short man who was at center stage wearing a bright pink suit that shimmered with rows of rhinestones. He was playing a guitar that was bigger than he was and singing a song about his mama. The stage manager pointed to the man and said, "That's Little Jimmy Dickens."

I leaned against the famous GooGoo candy bar placard for support and thanked the man with the headset. Then I asked, "And who am I?" He started to check his folded sheet of paper again, but before he could answer, I heard the voice of Little Jimmy Dickens saying something that sounded vaguely familiar, and then he said, "Ladies and gentlemen, please make welcome, for the first time on the Grand Ole Opry—Mrs. Chonda Pierce!"

The short man, who never stopped sparkling, smiled and nodded as he passed by me. (I'm almost certain I heard him ask the stage manager, "Now, who is she?") I stepped into the circle of light and across the same polished boards as did so many whom the world considers famous. But all thoughts of country music history had left me. I could think only of the little churches I had grown up in—several of them over the years—my mom and my dad, my brother and my sisters. I thought of all the stories I could tell. But then, of course, that's why I was there: I had a story to tell. It wasn't very long, and sometimes I didn't think it was an exciting story at all. But I've told it a lot. And the funny thing is—it seemed the more I told it, the more people wanted to hear it. Then one day someone from the Grand Ole Opry wanted me to share my story.

I almost felt I should have prepared something really special for such a big occasion. But I didn't. I just took a deep breath and began as I always have: "Hi. My name is Chonda. And I grew up in church—sitting on the second row, piano side . . ."

When we were growing up, we used to sing together all the time. We thought we were going to be a great singing quartet—all we needed was a bus. Mama used to dress us alike, and we'd sing and—well, it was hard on my brother, 'cause he was a boy.*

———————————————◆———————————————

1

The Singing Courtneys

FROM WHERE WE SAT, WE COULD *SEE* JUST ABOUT everything going on in church. We had a good view of Mom, who was playing the piano. In fact, we were close enough that we could discern just the slightest lifting of her brow, the sort of movement that told us all to be very, very still—or else. And we could see my father just as well on the platform, behind the pulpit. We were close enough to be frozen to our seats by a certain glare. Believe me—it wasn't our idea to sit where we sat. We longed for the freedom of the back row, out of range of Dad's glare and Mom's lifted brow.

From where we sat, we experienced things no one else could have. People came into our lives. Some stayed, and others just passed through, leaving their marks on us forever. Some things we saw were scary; some things were

*"The Singing Courtneys" by Chonda Pierce. © 1994 BMM Music. Used by permission. Gaither Copyright Management.

funny. Sometimes we hurt, and often we were comforted. Sometimes we were glad and even proud to sit where we sat; other times we longed to sit on that back row, like a visitor coming in late and sure to slip out early—not getting a really good look at anything.

There were four of us looking out over the church from our designated pew. Michael was seven years older than I. He wore dark-rimmed glasses, usually bandaged in the middle with tape because they had broken during one of his basketball games when he had forgotten to strap them to his head. Next was Charlotta. She was only a couple of years younger than Mike. She could play the piano, and she taught me things like which fork to use with the salad and which one to use with the meal. Then there was me.

Sometimes I wondered if Mom ever lifted her brow or Dad ever glared before I was born. I was about five years old when I was standing on my tiptoes to get a drink from the water fountain. It was between Sunday School and worship service, so the hallway was filled with folks heading to the sanctuary and others slipping out the side door for their cars. As I drank down the cool water, I could hear two grayheaded, been-around-for-years saints of the church whispering to one another as they slipped in line behind me. One patted me gently on the back of the head and said to her friend, "This is one of our preacher's daughters. She's not very p-r-e-t-t-y."

I turned around and in a matter-of-fact way answered, "No. But I'm real s-m-a-r-t." See what I mean?

And finally there was the baby of the family, Cheralyn. She was three years younger than I. She was quiet and reserved and compassionate enough that, if she had her way, every stray dog and cat in town would have taken *our* spot on *our* pew. The four of us made cute stairsteps—standing up or sitting down.

From our vantage point we had the opportunity to experience firsthand the good, the bad, and the ugly. In our world—the conservative Southern parsonage—we grew up rubbing elbows with the saints and the not-so-saintly Sunday after Wednesday after Sunday. Through it all a bond more powerful than death and more meaningful than life itself was forged—a strength that has survived some of the most bizarre moments found in the church, a force stronger than the cruelest and most self-righteous abuse sometimes found there, a ray of hope planted so deeply that we could look past the stained-glass jungle and see it for what it was meant to be all along. We could see all of this and more seated right there—on the *second row, piano side.*

My mother spent many long hours teaching us the strangest things. She wasn't satisfied to teach us just the kinds of things other mothers teach their children—things like *Eat all your carrots—they're good for your eyes;* or *Don't talk with your mouth full;* or *Don't make ugly faces at people, or your face will get stuck like that*—or *If the Lord had meant for you to have holes in your ears, He would have put them there!* (That was right up there with *Always wear clean underwear in case you're in a wreck!*)

---◆---

In our conservative Southern parsonage world, we grew up rubbing elbows with the saints and the not-so-saintly.

---◆---

Mom was also our drama coach, our piano teacher, and our own live-in Emily Post. All three of these areas were put to the ultimate test whenever the district superintendent scheduled a visit to our church and our home.

I was much too young to understand just what the responsibilities of a district superintendent were. All I knew was that when we heard that he and his wife were coming, we would spend countless hours cleaning floors, polishing furniture, washing windows—and then we'd start on the house! Oh, the endless amount of preparation for a fellow in a nice car and a new suit. I guess he was the nearest thing to being Dad's boss. *Roll out the red carpet, I'd think, because the Gospel Circus is about to begin!* (To this day I get tremendously nervous around district superintendents.)

On one particular visit, Mother had taught us all specific scripture verses to recite. We had our songs ready and our best Sunday clothes on. Our hair was combed and our smiles were fine-tuned, just in time for our traditional Sunday afternoon Gospel Music Show. I was given the honor of being the opening act. Mother had written a perfect poem for me to recite—I even had it memorized (not bad for a five-year-old). All the proper gestures had been rehearsed. Act One was about to begin.

My precious poem was supposed to be

> *We hope you like our singing.*
> *We're glad that you are here.*
> *We want to fill your visit*
> *With happiness and cheer!*

But something came over me. I couldn't help editing Mother's poem. Out of my mouth came

> *We hope you like our singing.*
> *We're glad that you are here.*
> *Now let's go in the kitchen*
> *And have a glass of beer!*

The show was over. Curtain closed!*

I suppose if it hadn't been for my mother's sincerity, I would have begun to think that church and religion were just something you did for show. We memorized scripture for everything—Bible quizzing, Vacation Bible School contests, Sunday School classes, to impress our grandparents and schoolteachers. We had a Sunday School chorus for every occasion. We all were taught the piano starting with "Snug as a Bug in a Rug." We moved on to "Amazing Grace" and eventually worked our way to "How Firm a Foundation." Inevitably, as the years passed, I began to question what *was* real and what was show.

*"Sunday Afternoon Gospel Show" by Chonda Pierce. © 1994 BMM Music. Used by permission. Gaither Copyright Management.

Unfortunately there was another show, a more painful one, that began to be played out in the parsonage family. We were living in Georgetown, South Carolina, when I began to notice my parents' sometimes rocky relationship. And the contrast I witnessed between our everyday life and the Sunday morning show was very confusing. I have always been bold enough—or stupid enough—to say what I think. Keeping *the secret* was especially hard for me. It is amazing that I didn't get slapped in the mouth more often than I did. But with the same discipline we were taught in learning our scriptures, we were also taught that there are some things you just don't talk about if you sit on the "second row, piano side."

Out of respect for others, the secrets of the second row should remain secret—secrets like the ones we overheard at home: whose kids were in trouble, who was struggling financially in the church, whose kids were flunking out of school, and who was getting a divorce and why. And although we would be privy to a few details that leaked out during our family devotions or dinner conversation, there was one secret we were very seldom privy to—our parents' marital problems. It amazes me that the full extent of my parents' painful relationship could have been kept so hush-hush. Even now I will not tell their story. I can only relate to you how life on the "second row, piano side" affected me.

We were taught that there are some things you just don't talk about if you sit on the "second row, piano side."

Despite the confusion and the secrets, somewhere during the course of all the talent contests, scripture memorization, recitals, and essay writings, a belief system was born. A single stone was laid. When I believed my mother to be laboring in the fields of arts and crafts by sewing costumes for Christmas plays, writing poems for special Sunday night services, sounding out the hard-to-read names from the Bible so that I could understand them, she was actually working as a stonemason, laying the solid, intricate teachings that would someday form a foundation.

Mom the bricklayer! There were no stories of babies who came from cabbage patches—babies came from Jesus. Easter was a celebration of new life—not just candy in baskets. Somehow even Santa Claus and Jesus Christ were best friends, and we believed it. There were no ridiculous theories that we evolved from some huge explosion in the sky—God put us here. Mother told us about the gospel. She read it to us. We memorized it. We believed it.

As I grew older, life's circumstances began to carve away at my faith. In my teens I began to search for answers. I wasn't particularly rebellious. It's just that the secrets I carried from the second row seemed to get heavier and heavier.

---◆---

I have an image of Mom now: mortar splattered across her apron, a trowel in one hand held loosely by fingers bruised from the countless stones it took to build sturdy foundations for four children.

---◆---

I was eight years of age when I memorized the Shepherd's Psalm and quoted it word for word to win a local talent contest. Regretfully, it wasn't until I was about 22 years old that I really came to know the Shepherd. I am so grateful to my mother for insisting that I learn that passage of scripture and even more grateful to the Holy Spirit, who helped me to understand and believe its meaning. What kinds of answers would I have found to my many questions if Mother had not laid these first stones? I have an image of Mom now: mortar splattered across her apron, a trowel in one hand held loosely by fingers bruised from the countless stones it took to build sturdy foundations for four children—children who eventually learned who the Shepherd is and the joy found in the fellowship of His faithful flock.

> The LORD is my shepherd; I shall not be in want.
>   He makes me lie down in green pastures,
> he leads me beside quiet waters,
>   he restores my soul.
> He guides me in paths of righteousness
>   for his name's sake.
> Even though I walk
>   through the valley of the shadow of death,
> I will fear no evil,
>   for you are with me;
> your rod and your staff,
>   they comfort me.
> You prepare a table before me
>   in the presence of my enemies.
> You anoint my head with oil;
>   my cup overflows.
> Surely goodness and love will follow me
>   all the days of my life,
> and I will dwell in the house of the LORD
>   forever.
>   —Ps. 23, author's paraphrase

Interlude

Garth and Pat

*A*ND, OH, BY THE WAY," *Bob Whitaker, my friend and manager of the Grand Ole Opry, called to remind me, "Your appearance with Garth Brooks will be on live TV. See you then."*

On live TV? With Garth Brooks? This would mean that during my five-minute performance the Opry would be filled to capacity with more than 5,000 Garth fans—waiting for the ditzy blond to get off the stage so they could see the real star. They would chant, "Garth! Garth! Garth!" as I would try to tell my stories from the second row, piano side! The estimated 40 million viewers watching the live program at home would all get up and go to the bathroom during my portion, grumbling with aggravation at the comedian who was taking up such precious airtime. And only a very small handful of my family would be huddled around a television set somewhere asking one another, "What did she say? Her name's not Garth! Why do they keep calling her Garth?"

I called my mother—as usual. She was so excited. She went on and on about what an outstanding opportunity this would be for me: the exposure, the blessing, the thrill of working with this entertainment icon. "Oh, Honey, this is wonderful!" she said. "But now tell me, who exactly is Garth Brooks?" Once again, without even realizing it, my mother had placed into perspective the things I needed to concentrate on and the things I shouldn't worry about.

I arrived at the Opry at my appropriate call time. Backstage was like a photographer's convention. This could mean only one thing: Mr. Brooks was in the building.

I stopped in the makeup room, sat in a chair, and chal-

lenged the ladies to make me look like a star. In the middle of a "coifing" the door opened, and without fanfare a young couple stepped into the room. The lady found a seat, and the man walked over to the chair beside me. He very calmly and politely slipped off his black cowboy hat, nodded, and introduced himself to me and the makeup ladies. We were all stunned, frozen—my hair not quite done. Garth Brooks! I should think of something really witty and clever to say, I thought. I should be aggressive and hand him my tape. I should borrow a few million dollars! But we just sat quietly in our makeup chairs as the room slowly filled with flash-bulbs of autograph-seekers (granted, one of those cameras was my own) and recording industry folks.

After a quick interview on the preview show, "Back Stage at the Opry," I slipped into my designated spot in the wings to wait for Johnny Russell to introduce me to the eager crowd. There was no entourage in my corner except for my husband and a few close friends. No flashbulbs, no auto-graph-seekers or recording industry folks—except for Norman Holland, my faithful friend from Chapel Records.

I made my way to center stage, took a deep breath, and started with a few stories from the second row. Amazingly enough, there were no "Garth" chants as I'd envisioned. They were politely attentive, and I think I even remember a chuckle or two (my husband used the word "guffaw" to describe their response). I said good-night, and Johnny Russell called me back out for a second bow when I noticed the quiet figure taking his place in preparation for his time in the spotlight. I passed through the crowd and mustered up enough nerve to shake his hand as he went by. I don't know if he ever saw my performance, but his kind smile seemed to tell me that every-thing was fine, that he'd been in those intimidating places, when your stomach is in knots and you think the world is not listening to what you have to say. He patted me on the back and stopped for a picture. I've never seen him again.

A few weeks later, a nearby television station, TBN, tele-phoned and invited me to appear on their Gospel America

Show. I recognized the host's name. I had seen him on a few gospel programs in the past. I loved his daughter's singing voice. And his films were cute. The show would be prerecorded, and there wouldn't be a live audience at all. I accepted and phoned Mother, as usual, to tell her the news.

I almost dropped the phone as she screamed with excitement on the other end. She knew exactly who the host was and insisted that I take her along. "This is truly a blessing," she said, "and he can sing rings around that Garth fella!" She couldn't wait for the chance to get his autograph. She started naming movie titles and singing songs to me on the phone. She went on and on about how handsome he was and about how "cool" his white patent leather shoes were. It was the perfect opportunity to ask, "Mom, now tell me—exactly who is Pat Boone?"

The U-Haul truck backed up to the front door, and while the workers took all our belongings inside and set them onto the floor of our new parsonage, we kids went next door to check out the new church. We found these little bitty drinking glasses. Then we went outside and set up two brick blocks with a plank across them and played Gunsmoke Saloon all day with Communion glasses—until the ladies' fellowship group came over with a covered dish. After they'd gone, my mother cried. I said, "Don't worry, Mom—we offered them a drink!" She didn't get it! We got *it* real good!*

---◆---

2

Aunt Doris, Aunt Doris

ROCK HILL, SOUTH CAROLINA, IS A SMALL TOWN snugly situated near the North Carolina state line. It was the site of my dad's first pastorate. We moved from Kentucky in 1964 and discovered a new church family. The church and the parsonage were side by side. I think the same contractor must have built both buildings; they looked almost identical. There was only one way to tell them apart: the church had a steeple, and the parsonage didn't!

Well, actually one night while Mom and Dad were on

*"The Communion Glasses" by Chonda Pierce. © 1994 BMM Music. Used by permission. Gaither Copyright Management.

visitation, we tried to burn down the parsonage. Mike and Charlotta carried Cheralyn and me into the hall closet to tell us ghost stories. The story was scary, but not as frightening as the sight of orange and yellow flames dancing up the sleeve of one of my mother's hanging coats. I suppose we shouldn't have lit those candles for special effect.

Charlotta carried Cheralyn, while Mike dragged me across the snow-covered front lawn to the house across the street to call the fire department. Luckily, the house suffered only minor smoke damage. My brother was the most exciting baby-sitter I'd ever had! Despite my vote of confidence, Mike was fired (no pun intended). It was a while before we were left alone again.

The church folks from Rock Hill provided my first experience with *a church family*—a family I'll never forget. I can still see Brother Pea, who always passed out dimes to the preacher's kids every Sunday morning. He'd once had skin cancer on his face, and consequently a portion of his cheek had been removed. The surgery had left a small opening about the size of a pea in his cheek. (I always wondered if that's where he got his name, but Mother wouldn't let me ask.) I also remember Grandma Simmons, who lived in a white house behind the church. She was the first "aisle runner" and "glory shouter" I ever knew. It just hadn't been a good revival if Grandma Simmons hadn't shouted and run the aisles—as a matter of fact, it just hadn't been a good church service without it either.

My most special memories in Rock Hill are of Aunt Doris. Every preacher's kid needs an *Aunt Doris*—especially a preacher's middle kid.

At that time in my life, I shared a bedroom with my two sisters. Charlotta had grace and talent on her side. Everyone seemed to dote over her long, blond hair (always curled in ringlets), her extraordinary musical abilities, and her sweet poise and manners. Cheralyn was the "baby." Need I say more? Who can compete with a baby? She toddled around our little home like she owned the place! She was remarkable—beautiful dark eyes, olive skin, yet with soft, bright blond hair. Her only physical flaw was her nose, which was always skinned up. But even that turned into her advantage. It just meant more lollipops at church and more to-do over her little "boo-boo"! And even though I idolized my brother, Mike, he was "too cool" to be seen with a kid sister.

But I had Aunt Doris. And Aunt Doris had me! She let me sleep over at her house—all by myself. She fixed my favorite foods and always seemed to have a little surprise in her purse at church—just for me. She would pick me up Saturday afternoons and take me to Rose's Department Store. There I could get a piece of candy (that I didn't have to share), a stick of bubble gum, and ride the electric pony—all for a nickel!

Aunt Doris was not related to my family, but going to her house anytime was as wonderful to me as going to Grandma's house at Christmastime. She was special. And she was my Sunday School teacher. Aunt Doris made me feel as if I were the most important little girl in the world.

I ran into Aunt Doris a few years ago. My heart jumped. All it took was her sweet arms around my adult shoulders for me to feel like that special little girl again! We reminisced about our Rock Hill church family. I was so happy to be able to introduce her to my daughter. I wanted somehow for that same magic that was poured out onto me to flow onto *my* little girl. As we drove away, I quietly prayed for the Lord to please send my daughter an "Aunt Doris"—someone who would boost her morale and take her on fun trips to the department store; someone who would be a pal; someone who could make her feel important and special.

I thank God for every Aunt Doris in our lives. For Charlotta it was a nice man in Georgetown who bought her a piano when he noticed her natural ability in music. For Cheralyn it was a family who had a farm on the edge of town and gave her a Shetland pony when they saw her compassion for animals. These generous gifts were wonderful. They were sincere expressions of love from people who had invested time in getting to know the preacher's kids. Their commitment inspired us to see all that is good in a church family.

**Aunt Doris was as busy as anyone else.
Yet she found time to minister to
one little skinny kid.**

I always marvel at the many excuses I hear around church for not getting involved. Life *is* complicated now. People are working long hours, paying bills, and caring for elderly parents. People have huge responsibilities that occupy their minds and their time. Aunt Doris had all those things too. Yet somehow she allowed the Lord to use her talents to minister to just one little skinny kid. Aunt Doris never sang in the choir, played the piano, or painted gorgeous paintings for the church foyer. But she used the gifts she had. She encouraged. She loved. She baked cookies. She kept a piece of candy in her pocket. She remembered birthdays. She gave great hugs and warm kisses. *That's* talent.

Years later my brother, Mike, did me a great favor without realizing it: he married a sweet girl named Doris. My sister-in-law is now that special aunt to my children. And whenever we're together and I hear that familiar phrase roll off my children's tongues: *"Aunt Doris, can we . . . ?"* I thank God for now and for then.

Thank you, Aunt Doris.

Interlude

⸺⸺⸺◆⸺⸺⸺

Comic Belief

I WAS SITTING IN A HOTEL ROOM IN INDIANAPOLIS when I called back home to check on the kids. They were fine. My husband, David, told me that Norman Holland was trying to get in touch with me. He had left several numbers, so it sounded as if it must be pretty important. Norman has been one of the most important influences in my career. At this time he was the artist and relations director for Riversong Records, the Southern Gospel division at Benson Records.

Norman is the type of man who will tell it to you straight—no fluff, no beating around the bush. He always advised me from his heart. He believed in me long before I was believing in myself. He gave me my first opportunity to see my cassette in a Christian bookstore when I was on a comedy series for Riversong. He became my friend, so when he calls and leaves several numbers by which to track him down, I do just that.

I found Norman at home that evening. He told me he had passed my cassette on to a friend of his—Mark Lowry. And Mark was putting together a tour called Comic Belief. It seemed he wanted to know if I'd be interested in traveling with several Christian comedians for about 20 appearances.

Three comedians on one bus? I thought. We'll kill each other! I had apprehensions about leaving home for such a long period of time. Mr. Ward assured me that they would be weekend engagements until the spring, and by that time, we could make some arrangements with the family. He told me Mark was tickled to have me come to work for him. He discussed my salary and product information. There would be

27

Comic Belief T-shirts, baseball caps, pictures, and so on. I could just imagine standing in an auditorium working all night selling *Mark Lowry* T-shirts and videos—I mean, I'd really wanted to meet him and all, but I just wasn't interested in sales work.

Mr. Ward started laughing, and he complimented my wit. (I don't think he ever realized I was serious!) I never was really sure what I would be doing on the *Comic Belief* Tour until we left Nashville one morning and headed for Anderson, Indiana, for our first concert. I was so nervous. I tried not to let on—never let them see you sweat!

The parking lot of the church was filled with cars. We slipped into the back door, and I was quickly introduced to Mark Steele. I shook his hand. Our little meeting room was quiet. (I learned the hard way that Mr. Lowry likes peace and quiet before a concert: "Inside voice, Chonda," Mark would say. "Inside voice.")

I didn't think things could get any more awkward until Mark said, "Well, guys, some friends of mine are here. I've asked one of them to pop in and have prayer with us." About that time the door flew open as kids ran and jumped all over Mark Lowry. He laughed and tickled each one of them. He asked, "Where's your mom?"

"Here I am!" came a voice that was strangely familiar. In a moment Sandi Patty appeared.

My chin dropped. (For a split second it was as big as Mark Lowry's!) I sat there quietly, trying to pretend this stuff happens to me all the time. We all bowed our heads to pray—and as soon as we said, "Amen," I stuck my hand out, introduced myself, and asked for her autograph. She kindly obliged. When she left the room, Mark Lowry began the business meeting with, "Well, ya'll—what do you want to do tonight?"

We shrugged and responded really businesslike: "We dunno. Whad'ya want us to do?"

He gave us just a few instructions. Mark Steele was to go first, then me, then Mark Lowry would go until intermission. We would come back on as he reintroduced us for the second half. He told me, "Chonda, I've heard your tape, and I *want you to speak from your heart the second half. You have an incredible testimony these folks need to hear. Oh, and by the way, during the first half, try to be funny!" He grinned.*

That was the longest night of my performing life. About five minutes into my portion, I glanced across the crowd as I told my stories from the second row—and there on about the 12th row were Bill and Gloria Gaither and their grandchildren. A couple of rows back from them was Sandi Patty and her kids. Jerry Falwell was closer to the front. My knees knocked together. I worried about fainting.

The night mercifully ended. I waited quietly on the bus. I was sure Mark would say, "Well, we gave it a shot. I'll send you a check. Keep trying." But not a word.

Our 20 planned concerts turned into 50, and before we had finished we had done nearly 70. The Comic Belief Tour lasted almost 18 months. During that time, several different comedians worked on the tour. Mark Steele was fabulous. Paul Aldrich brought the house down with "Jesus in the '90s!" And Joe Gautier left the audience screaming in laughter at "Give Tanks!" I shared my stories from the second row, piano side, and closed every evening with a word of testimony just before Mark would end the evening with a song and a prayer. I am convinced not only that Comic Belief was a successful tour from a business standpoint but also that God blessed our efforts and used the laughter, the music, and the stories to touch hearts and to change lives.

I am grateful to Mark Lowry for the invitation to participate in such an exciting venture. Mark is the paragon of success in Christian comedy. No one comes close to his expertise. Tens of thousands of people have listened to him and laughed, and many of those have found the joy of salvation.

Mark has been a mentor and friend. I have never heard him say an unkind word, make a judgmental statement, or criticize anyone. He has been tremendously complimentary of what I do. His influence and recommendations have opened many doors for me. And it was months before I had the nerve to say to audiences, "We travel in two buses—one for the comedians and one for Mark's chin."

> Our favorite thing to do on Easter Sunday was to see what the rich kids were wearing—'cause we knew that's what we'd be wearing the next Easter.

———————◆———————

3

The Lemonade Stand

ALONG WITH SCRIPTURE VERSES, CHORUSES, manners, and the proper dress code, the greatest thing my mother passed on to us was the gift of adaptation. I am almost certain that my mother invented the phrase "When life gives you lemons . . ." Mom and Dad instilled in us not only the joy of a good glass of lemonade but also the thrill of making it yourself!

We never considered ourselves well-off financially. We seldom considered ourselves poor. We simply didn't consider *ourselves*. My wardrobe was filled with hand-me-downs and homemade dresses my grandmother would send us every fall for the upcoming school year. When we wore shoes, they were usually tennis shoes or sandals. Since we lived in the South, barefoot was vogue!

———————◆———————

"Mom, who could need 'em worse than us?"

———————◆———————

There did come a brief time when the realization that "We *are* poor" hit us all. Mother couldn't find a job. Dad had just accepted a call to a small church in Orangeburg, South Carolina. Mike had gone to a college 500 miles away, and Charlotta was soon to follow. I can remember hearing Mom and Dad argue about the possibility of getting food stamps. I don't think it was as much a matter of pride as it was that Mom still didn't consider us desperate enough. She would say, "But what if someone else needs them more?"

As I sat at the dinner table eating for the fifth time that week a sandwich made with government cheese and grilled with government butter, I looked at her and said, "Mom, who could need 'em worse than us?"

So one afternoon Mom and I stood in the food stamp line for more than three hours. Of course, after we got them, the whole family wanted in on the selection process at the grocery store. Grocery shopping had never been so exciting. Everyone was thrilled to pick out the food, but as soon as we approached the checkout counter, they all scrambled to the car—except for Mom and me. When Mother handed the girl at the Piggly Wiggly our little booklet, I grinned at Mother and said in my most Southern-belle, Scarlet O'Hara voice, "I'll tell the driver to bring the limo around, Mother, and pick us up at the door. I know how you hate to wait in this summer heat." When the food stamps ran out, we went back to grilled cheese until things began to pick up at the church again.

Mother had toyed a long time with the idea of going to nursing school. When she heard that Baptist Hospital in Columbia, South Carolina, was offering a two-year Licensed Practical Nurse (LPN) course, she decided that this would be the year. She and Dad argued about her decision for hours— but for some reason, Mother truly felt nursing school was something she was called to do. She borrowed the money from her mother, and at the age of 40 off to school she went.

She drove 91 miles round trip to nursing school every day. Cheralyn and I made flash cards and quizzed her for exams. She amazed us all. Mother had not been in school in 22 years and would have failed chemistry in high school twice had it not been for the tutor her mom and dad had hired during her senior year. She passed nursing school with flying colors, and we proudly attended her graduation from LPN school. (Dad had refused to attend—but near the end of the ceremony we noticed him on the back row of that huge auditorium in Columbia.)

While Mom was in nursing school, Cheralyn and I had almost full responsibility of the house. We had our regular chores to do as well as cooking most of the meals. We were proud of our diverse menus: macaroni and cheese, peanut butter and jelly, Froot Loops—and on special occasions (or Friday, whichever came first) *hot dogs!*

Did I mention that we lived on a tight budget? We had a few poundings from the church folks—but you get mostly dusty, dented cans of yams and cranberry sauce at those things! So Cheralyn and I decided the answer to our menu problem was simply to grow our own garden. We worked for hours getting the soil ready. We saved our money and went down to the local hardware store and purchased seed packets of green beans, corn, cucumbers, and tomatoes. The weeds outgrew our patience, and our sandy Southern soil could produce nothing—nothing but cucumbers, that is.

They were everywhere! We had a long vine of cucumbers that stretched from the front porch of our house, across the church parking lot, and up the steps of the fellowship hall. We made cucumber sandwiches, cucumber salad, fried cucumbers—anything you could make with cucumbers, we made. Some things you couldn't make with cucumbers we made anyway. And we ate them all.

Then just like the plagues finally ended in Egypt, we received a sweet reprieve from our cucumber suppers. A man in our church raised hogs for his chain of barbecue restaurants. He called the house one evening to say that the next morning he would be stopping by with a package for the pastor and his family. Hallelujah!

Cheralyn and I rewrote our menu for the next month:

barbecued pork chops, ribs, ham, bacon—we even made plans for the ears and the feet. We set the table that night for tomorrow's dinner. We were so excited we could hardly sleep. (Or maybe it was the cucumbers!)

———◆———

Cheralyn and I rewrote our menu for the next month: barbecued pork chops, ribs, ham, bacon—we even made plans for the ears and the feet.

———◆———

Nevertheless, as promised, an old pickup truck pulled into the driveway the next afternoon. A kind old farmer climbed out of his truck carrying a huge package wrapped in brown paper. The front of his apron was bloody, but we hardly pitied the beast we would dine on for the next few weeks. We could smell something spicy and delicious as he set the package on the counter. We had envisioned a huge country ham, perhaps a pork roast, maybe slabs of bacon. We couldn't wait for him to leave so we could dive in.

Mother thanked him very kindly, and as the front door clicked shut, Cheralyn and I ripped open our mouth-watering feast. There it was—a fresh, meaty, 15-pound roll of *bologna!* Now don't get me wrong. I don't dislike bologna. But a couple of skinny little preacher's kids had waited all day long for pork chops and had gotten bologna—disappointing bologna.

When mother fixed supper that night, we were surprised to see something shaped like pork chops on our plates. Mother had used some of her arts and crafts skills to cut little pork chop shapes out of the bologna and fried it until it was crisp. Served with cold, sliced cucumbers and cornbread, Mom showed us how to make lemonade out of lemons.

The next day the doorbell rang. A young lady stood on our porch and explained to Mother how she had noticed the church next door and wondered if we knew how to reach the pastor. Mother invited her in. With watery eyes, she told Mother that her children were hungry and that her husband had been out of work for several months. Her food stamps had run out too. Without question, Mom quickly filled a grocery sack with cucumbers and cut our much-needed roll of bologna in half and shared it with this stranger. They shared a glass of lemonade before she left, and we never saw her again.

> *Be kind and compassionate to one another,*
> *forgiving each other,*
> *just as in Christ God forgave you.*
>
> —Eph. 4:32

Interlude

———————————◆———————————

Answer the Phone, Please

*O*NE MORNING MARK LOWRY CALLED *and said in his normal mature voice, "Na-na-na—I know something you don't know! Somebody's gonna call you—and I'm not telling you who it is! Na-na-na-na!" Now, who could he possibly know who would call me and cause me to shout and run the aisles? I asked myself.*

It was early Monday morning. I made myself forget about what Mark had said; otherwise I wouldn't be able to move about my day without jumping out of my skin whenever the phone rang. I had started a load of laundry and noticed my son playing outside in his pajamas, getting his usual early start in the tree house. I stepped outside to tell Zachary to come down and eat his breakfast and get some clothes on. He answered, "I'm not hungry, and I've got some clothes on." He's quick. (I remember when I was five and had a good time in my pajamas.)

I noticed that Spot, our dalmatian (the children are so creative with their pet names too), was standing rather anxiously beside his empty bowl (he's as subtle as Mark Lowry). So I told Zach as we stepped inside the back door to bring me the box of Gravy Train out of the laundry room. When I turned to shut the door, I noticed it. Like a beacon flashing an SOS from a nearby lighthouse, the message light on the answering machine was flashing! The phone must have rung while I was outside retrieving Zach and saving Spot from starvation! (Or was that the other way around?)

I pressed the button to see who had called. I stopped breathing until the message was long over: "Chonda? This is

35

Carolyn at Bill Gaither's office. He was calling to chat with you. Would you please return his call at your convenience at area code . . ."

I could have kicked myself and the dog! I couldn't believe I missed it!

I ran to the phone, taking the handoff of Gravy Train from Zachary on the way by. He sat down at the table and said, "OK, Mom, now I'm hungry. Can I have some Captain Crunch?"

"Sure, Sweetie," I said. (He hates it when I call him sweetie!) "Let me make a phone call, Zachary. This is a very important man. I'll only be a minute." I wanted him to know how important this call was to Mommy. (I remember when I was five and hungry.)

With unsteady hands, I dialed the number and asked for Carolyn. She politely said, "Oh, dear—he just stepped out for a breakfast meeting. I'll have him call you the minute he gets in. He's anxious to talk to you. We've all heard so much about you."

I couldn't believe it. Bill Gaither had heard about me? (Well, Mark does have a big mouth, thank the Lord!) I was so excited. I hung up the phone and called my mother, my brother, my husband—and about three cousins. I poured Zachary's breakfast and helped him into some play clothes. I couldn't imagine what Bill Gaither would be calling me about. Just a kind word of encouragement from him, I thought, would be enough to keep me working hard for the next 10 years. I slipped out to the backyard to fill Spot's doggie bowl. As I opened the box and began to pour, I gasped! I quickly ran back into the house just as Zachary lifted his cereal spoon to his mouth. "Wait, Zach! Mom messed up— that's Spot's Gravy Train! Your Captain Crunch is in Spot's bowl. We'll have to start all over."

"Or we could just trade seats!" Zach said. (I told you he was quick.)

I stepped outside again, apologized to Spot, and gave him his Gravy Train. I stepped back in, and Zach said, "Telephone was ringing, Mom."

I raced to the answering machine and punched the flashing light: "Chonda? This is Carolyn. Looks like we've missed you again. Please call when you can!"

I called back immediately this time, pushed the wrong buttons, and had to start over twice. Finally Carolyn answered, "Chonda? Oh, I'm sorry. Mr. Gaither is on another line. It's long distance, and he could be awhile. Looks like you two will be playing phone tag all day." He could call me later. But just in case, I told her I'd call back after I took Zachary to kindergarten.

About an hour had gone by. I could have gotten back sooner, but I went to Wal-Mart and bought a cordless phone. Then I took a few minutes extra to log in Bill Gaither's number into the speed dial section. No more excuses! Part of me was beginning to wonder if Mark Lowry hadn't hired someone to sit at this phone number all day and pretend to be Carolyn.

I got comfortable on my couch, held my breath, and pushed speed dial number two. (Mom was number one, and I was going to call her next. Mark was number three, just in case this was just a sick joke of his.) The lady who called herself Carolyn answered again. "I'm sorry. You just missed him again. And it looks like he'll be out for the rest of the day." I was about to hang up, take a stab at number "three," and get to the bottom of this when Carolyn said, "But he did ask me to ask if you would be available to come to Praise Gathering in Indianapolis in October."

I didn't say, "Let me check my calendar" or even "Let me get back with you." Without trying to sound too excited or anxious, I said calmly and simply, "You better believe it!"

I never did get to talk with Bill Gaither on the phone. But what a thrill it was to shake his hand and talk with him at Praise Gathering. He handed me the microphone and patted my shoulder as he introduced me to his audience on that first night. After I had shared a few stories from the second row, piano side, along with a few words of testimony, I sang a song dedicated to my mother, "Somebody's Praying."

More than 12,000 people rose to their feet and gave me a standing ovation as I handed the microphone back to Mr. Gaither. He just grinned. I found some new friends that night. Bill and Gloria Gaither were real. Encouraging. Approachable. They have believed in me and have watched me grow as a performer. They are "second row" friends.

I ran into Mark Lowry in the hallway after the evening service. As always, he was a proud big brother. As always, he said in his usual mature way, "Na-na-na-na—I knew it before you did!"

I went to youth camp for the first time when I was 12. Mom tried to get them to take me sooner, but they wouldn't. I remember she packed all my clothes so nicely in my suitcase. She labeled each outfit "Monday," "Tuesday," "Wednesday," . . . wasn't that good? When I got back the next week, she opened my suitcase and there they were: "Monday," "Tuesday," "Wednesday" . . . I said, "Mom, it looked so nice, I didn't want to mess anything up." I wondered why no one had wanted to sit next to me at services that week.*

———————————◆———————————

4

Seashells and Cowboy Boots

ALTHOUGH I WAS BORN IN KENTUCKY, I WILL ALWAYS consider South Carolina home. After Rock Hill, Georgetown, and Orangeburg, we moved to Myrtle Beach, where for almost five years we could step out onto our porch and see the far horizon of the Atlantic Ocean whenever we wanted. We didn't eat a lot of shrimp—we fished with it off the Fourth Avenue Pier. We hardly noticed how salty the air was, because we were too busy building sand castles on Saturday afternoons.

We had memories of beached turtles, playing Frisbee

*"Youth Camp" by Chonda Pierce. © 1994 BMM Music. Used by permission. Gaither Copyright Management.

in the calm inlet waters, surfing, passing out the Four Spiritual Laws booklets with Youth for Christ while wearing swimsuits (Mom never did get used to that!), air-brushed T-shirts, tourists in shorts at church, Grand Stand hot dogs, hash on rice, boiled peanuts, gumbo, and shark's teeth. I don't dare forget the shark's teeth.

Cheralyn and I would spend hours on the beach. During low tide certain areas had fewer tourists and more sharks' teeth. We would take our finds to the Gay Dolphin Gift Cove, where we'd sell our sharks' teeth and sand dollars for enough money to buy Cokes and candy at the snack shop during youth camp.

Dad was doing a great job. The attendance in Sunday School had grown so much that we had to convert the parsonage into Sunday School space and move into a little brick house a few blocks away. The thought of leaving Myrtle Beach had never entered our minds.

I think it was Mother who broke the news to me that we were moving. We were aware that with Dad's line of work there was always that possibility. The move from Myrtle Beach was devastating for me. I had found my best lifelong girlfriend in Myrtle Beach. Donna Thompson and I had spent hours, weeks, and months playing "Mod Squad" and sending each other secret-coded notes in our lockers at school. I had my first date and my first broken heart in South Carolina. I had fallen in love for the first time at South Carolina youth camp, and then again at Teen-a-rama, and then again at the district Valentine's banquet, and then again on the IMPACT Team. Boy, did I love South Carolina!

Nevertheless, the decision to move had been announced, and our protests were ineffective. When I stepped out onto our front porch that night, I noticed, for the first time in five years, just how salty the evening air was.

Ashland City, Tennessee. The name sounded so boring when compared to Myrtle Beach. Tennessee? No one wore sandals in Tennessee. We liked rice at every meal; they ate potatoes. Tennesseans lived in flannel shirts and cowboy boots; we liked to ride motorcycles and dune buggies.

As we pulled our little caravan into the city limits of Ashland City, Mother drove the family car loaded with our clothes. Charlotta drove her car filled with dishes. Dad drove the U-Haul truck, and Mike drove the van loaded with one French poodle (Tippy), one German shepherd (Lady), three goldfish (nameless), one Shetland pony (Sugarfoot), and only two windows (and one of those was jammed and wouldn't roll down)! It was a small town with a beautiful courthouse in the middle of four streets they called "the square." Two traffic lights. One hamburger drive-in and one five-and-dime department store, aptly named Ashland City Department Store.

The biggest plus that Ashland City had going for it was that Mike and Charlotta were just 40 miles away now—at Trevecca Nazarene College in Nashville. That year Cheralyn became a cheerleader for the junior varsity basketball team. And I started my sophomore year in high school and fell in love for the first time—again—with a boy named Butch. (What else? We were in Tennessee now.)

I was not just thin—I was sickly looking! My hair frizzed at the slightest hint of rain. Mother had insisted that I needed a perm. It was supposed to thicken my hair so I'd look like a real teenager. Wrong! It earned me the nickname "Tweety Bird."

————————◆————————

Our drama teacher, Joyce Mayo, took a special interest in Cheralyn and me. We were accused of being the teacher's pets. We wore the reputation proudly.

————————◆————————

By the end of Christmas break, Butch was history and I was in love with a boy named Kevin. My hair had relaxed a little, and I had found a happy home in the drama department at Cheatham County High School. Along with the drama department came the greatest influence on my performing career as well as my education—Mrs. Joyce Mayo, my speech and drama teacher.

Mrs. Mayo seemed to take a special interest in Cheralyn and me. We performed for every variety show and had the leading roles in every play. We were accused of being the teacher's pets. We wore the reputation proudly. It was obvious by the prayers Mrs. Mayo rebelliously prayed aloud in class and the tears she sweetly shed with discouraged classmates that she and God had quite an important thing going on between them. Perhaps the Lord sent Mrs. Mayo along because He knew just what was ahead for these two frail girls, and He knew we'd need another Aunt Doris to help us get through. To this day I am grateful for having been a student and friend of my "drama mama"!

I am also grateful to Cheatham County High School and my 10th grade speech class for another very special reason. It was in that class that I noticed the dark, curly-haired boy who sat right behind me: David "the Ace" Pierce. He was always courteous but cool, made straight A's but was not a nerd. He was a champion wrestler for our high school team, played baseball, and liked the guitar. He was a little on the short side but gorgeous, soft-spoken yet tremendously funny. He became the best friend I ever had. And for the first time in my life I discovered the difference in having a crush on someone and being in love. (Kevin who?)

Interlude

♦

Live TV! Technical Difficulties

ONE AFTERNOON I STOOD IN THE KITCHEN *with a greasy mixture of ground beef, crackers, tomato paste, and onions oozing between my fingers. My hands were completely coated with the ingredients of my great-grandmother's meat loaf recipe when the telephone rang. With my left pinkie I answered it and balanced the receiver between my cheek and shoulder (a technique I hope to pass on to my great-grandchildren). It was Tandy Rice, a country music manager and mentor. He said, "Can you get ready in an hour?" Without waiting for an answer he went on to explain, "A limo will pick you up and take you to the Owen's Studio downtown. They want you to be on 'Crook and Chase' tonight. It's live TV with approximately 30 million viewers."*

I looked at the goo on my hands and glanced at my reflection on the oven door and said, "Sure! No problem."

I hung up the phone. What have I done? I thought. I'm not ready for this. I'm not live-TV funny. I'm scared to death. And then, glancing into the bathroom mirror, I screamed.

I set up the ironing board and turned on the bath water all in one quick motion. I ran to the phone, called my husband, David, and said, "Honey, get home quick!" Then I went back and wiped the hamburger goo off the ironing board, bathtub handles, and telephone.

As I took the last hot roller out of my hair, it dawned on me: TNN! None of my family had cable television! I called mother and told her. She was ecstatic and said she'd take a blank videotape to her neighbor. Of course, one call to Mother and I knew that in a matter of minutes every relative of

43

mine would soon be getting the news—and they did. We arranged for a friend to take Chera and Zachary to Vacation Bible School.

Sure enough, in about an hour a limo stopped outside our home. It was a white stretch limo complete with track lighting, tinted glass, a television set, and a wet bar in the corner. We climbed in quickly but not before some of the neighbor children could gather around and chase us down the street, waving and screaming, causing their parents to come out and stare and point.

We sat frozen in awe behind the tinted glass. Then David and I laughed at ourselves. It looked as if we were finally going to the prom together!

Suddenly a panicked expression washed over David's face. He leaned across the long seat and whispered, "Do you have any money?" I searched my purse and pockets and came up with $3.24. David searched his wallet and found a five-dollar bill. Oh my goodness—$8.24! How much do you tip a limo driver who drives you from Smyrna, Tennessee, to downtown Nashville and back again? Probably more than $8.24!

We arrived at the TV studio nervous and flustered. A nice lady led us down the hallway. She directed David to the men's room. (All of a sudden he wasn't feeling well. He kept asking me if I felt OK.) The same lady escorted me into a room that said "MAKEUP" on the door. I slipped into the chair she pointed to, and immediately another woman began to fuss over my hair, apply lipstick and powder, and whip me into shape for the bright lights and live cameras.

The guest celebrity was led in and sat in the chair next to me. I almost laughed out loud when I saw who it was. My, how time flies in Music City! A few months earlier I was pouring his coffee and typing lyric sheets that he had scribbled out on napkins. He was a songwriter friend I had met a couple of years before—Aaron Tippin. He was now traveling with an entourage of press people, fans, and band members. He was a star. He was as shocked to see me as I was to see him.

I was almost red-faced when I told him I was a comedian now. He laughed and said, "That figures—what happened?"

I knew what he was talking about. One day I had just walked into my boss's office and told her, "I have to go home."

She said, "OK, when will you be back?"

I said, "Probably never."

I didn't burn too many bridges; I just threw away the map that told me where they were.

But Aaron had noticed that I had disappeared. I told him I had begun a career in Christian comedy about a year earlier and that God was really blessing my work.

Enough said. When you need the conversation to clean up, clear out, or end, you need only to mention one of the three magic words—"Christian," "God," or "blessing" (I'd used all three)—and you get a quick, "Oh . . . I see . . ."

A man with headphones came and got me during a commercial break. We walked past the green room, and I saw David. He didn't look too good.

The man walked me to an "X" marked on the floor and said, "Start right here. Watch me for time and cues. Talk to the camera with the red light on. Move to the green (I briefly thought of my husband) "X" when camera-left comes on. You've got four minutes. During the applause, walk to the couch and shake Charley's hand in—" he checked his watch "5—4—3 [Your left or my left?] 2—1."

I heard a brief introduction faintly in the background. I think someone said my name. The lights came on, and the man with the headphones pointed at me.

I opened my mouth and began to speak, but I can't remember a word I said. At the end of the four minutes (and during an applause that surprised me), I walked to the couch, sat down, and chatted with Charlie Chase about comedy, Minnie Pearl, high school, and Opryland. We chuckled, we slapped each other's backs, he mentioned my tape, we went to a commercial break, and it was over.

The headphoned man met me at the couch, shook my

hand, and thanked me for coming. But before I left the stage area, I remembered! I ran back to the set, shook Charlie's hand again, and whispered in his ear, "Are we supposed to tip that limo driver or not?"

He laughed, said I was just a delight, and told the audience to give me a hand for my first live TV experience.

He thought I was joking! What was I going to tell David?

We climbed back into the limo. But by now David (whose color was coming back nicely) had devised a plan. He asked the driver if he could swing by the church so we could pick up our children. He honored our request and had to use the whole church parking lot just to turn the car around. The church family surrounded the car. Some of the children climbed in and all through the limo. They thought it was cute to take turns standing up through the skylight and waving at us. The limo driver took this opportunity to hand out business cards. David cornered the preacher, and I could see that money was changing hands.

We emptied the car of everyone but our family and headed for the short trip home. The driver seemed almost sad to leave, but I had a meat loaf to finish. Chera and Zach enjoyed the ride home. I hope the driver enjoyed his $18.24 tip.

And we'd play church for hours. My older sister, Charlotta, would play the piano (since she was the only one who knew how). She'd play 47 verses of "Mary Had a Little Lamb," and we'd sing 'em every one.

◆

5

Charlotta Kay—Half Flower Child, Half Missionary

THREE YEARS BEFORE I WAS EVER THOUGHT OF, Charlotta Kay was born—on May 10, my mother's birthday. I'm not sure whether it was that she and Mother shared a birthday or because she was mother's first girl that made them exceptionally close. And why not? To all of us, Sis was perfect!

Don't get me wrong. We had our share of squabbles. She seldom let me borrow her clothes or jewelry. She got to wear makeup (just a little), which only accented my plainness. She got to go on dates while I stayed home and washed the dishes—when it was *her* turn!

But Charlotta was everything that Cheralyn and I longed to be when we grew up. She was tall, beautiful, graceful, mannerly, and popular. On a typical afternoon, Sis would do our nails, fix our hair, and then have miniseminars on the proper way to set a table and eat spaghetti. (Even I, the tomboy, had fun taking Sis's etiquette lessons.) And once in a while, when she was sure that no one was looking, Sis would even play Barbies with us or make believe that she was the stewardess on the "Love Boat." Sis was cool.

She could play the piano and outsing Karen Carpenter any day. Under her direction, we became our small-town version of the Lennon Sisters. We entered dozens of talent contests. Charlotta would play the piano, and we'd sing a medley she had whipped together for the occasion. Our standard patriotic medley would bring home a trophy and prize money just about every time. (We'd leave the audience standing—or saluting.) We never squabbled over the trophy, just put it on the shelf with the rest of them. But squabbling over what toppings on the pizza we bought with our prize money would get us grounded every time!

On the spiritual continuum, Charlotta was somewhere between a flower child and a missionary. She was a thinker—a dreamer. She always reached out to the underdog. She repeatedly attached herself to the fellow in town everyone else had given up on. Most of the time these relationships ended, leaving her brokenhearted and carrying lifelong burdens. She carried scars from a few of these lost loves—scars I never knew existed.

"There is no hope," was once the thought I had.
No hope for me, no hope for you, no hope for love,
or anything else.
I gave up trying to win people's love or trying to
make people happy.
I just gave up on everything.
My life became an existence.
I did not live, I did not love, I merely was.
Then I turned. I turned to Jesus.
I found Him standing close by.
In a moment with my eyes in His direction,
I found hope;
I found answers,
I found life!
—Charlotta Kay Courtney
February 2, 1976

I'll never forget the day I met Paul Wayne Michael. I could tell by the glow on Charlotta's face and the gleam in his eyes that this was not the ordinary Friday night date. Paul Wayne was immediately one of us—not an outsider passing by or a project Charlotta had taken on to salvage. He was a breath of new life for Charlotta and another big brother for Cheralyn and me. Charlotta announced to us that she intended to marry Paul Wayne; the entire family was thrilled. No one worried that she was too young at the age of 20. They simply seemed right for each other. Paul Wayne loved her. We knew it, and that made us all happy.

We were in the midst of choir rehearsals with a community youth choir that Charlotta had put together in our little town. Costumes had been made (red, white, and blue), lines had been memorized, banners had been painted, and the choir was to debut its rendition of "Ring All the Bells of Freedom" at the county bicentennial celebration on July 4, 1976.

On July 3 Charlotta got dressed for work. She came into our room, kissed us good-bye, and reminded us of a few chores to do in preparation for that afternoon's concert. She had a busy day ahead of her at work and needed Cheralyn and me to help fold programs. We didn't mind her instructions. She had just moved back home a few weeks before, because she was trying to save money for her wedding. We knew it was temporary, but we were thrilled to have her home.

It had begun raining very heavily as she dashed to her car and drove toward the city to be at work by 8 A.M. Meanwhile, Cheralyn and I had a bowl of cereal together. Mother kept her usual Saturday appointment at the beauty shop. I worked part-time at my cousin's insurance office, answering the phone. So after Dad dropped me off at Huff Insurance, he drove mother to the Cut-n-Curl.

The phone was ringing when I unlocked the office door that morning. Cheralyn's shaken voice was on the other end. She wanted to know where Mom and Dad were. She said the county sheriff was at the house looking for Dad. He had told her that the highway patrol had telephoned, reporting that one of the Courtney children had been in an accident. I told her not to worry, that I would find Dad and get him the message. My hands were shaking as I dialed the number for the Cut-n-Curl. My mind began to race: *It was Michael. He was working as a youth pastor at a nearby church and had taken off on a camping trip on his motorcycle. Mother had begged him not to go. Why hadn't he listened? But Mike was six feet tall and 24 years old. For crying out loud, Mike—why couldn't you have been more careful?*

I remember my voice cracking and my heart pounding when I asked the receptionist at the beauty shop if I could speak to Rev. Courtney or his wife. I could picture Michael handcuffed to some patrol car, under arrest for reckless driving, blood running down the side of his face, then standing in a hospital hallway. I kept thinking, *I hope he's not hurt too bad, 'cause Dad is going to kill him. I wonder who'll have to pay for the messed-up motorcycle? Man—he can forget ever driving another bike of any kind. Mom's gonna have a fit!*

Mother picked up the phone, and before I could say anything, she instructed, "Chonda, lock the office and wait for your father and me out on the sidewalk. We need to take you home while we go into the city."

Cheralyn and I sat on the living room couch and waited and waited for Mother and Dad to make the drive into Nashville to find out what was going on at General Hospital. I tried to reassure Cheralyn that everything was going to be fine. I sat down at the piano and began to play the first song I turned to in a huge book sitting there. The corner of the page was turned down where Charlotta had marked this very song for last Wednesday night's prayer meeting. Cheralyn and I began to hum the tune before breaking into the chorus together:

> *For whatever it takes to draw closer to You, Lord,*
> *That's what I'll be willing to do.*

50

For whatever it takes to be more like You,
*That's what I'll be willing to do.**

Charlotta had sung so beautifully at church a few nights before. During the second verse, she stopped playing and put her head down on the piano and sobbed. She stood and testified to the congregation that she wanted to have prayer around the altar before she finished these words. Several ladies gathered around her. The Holy Spirit breezed across her thin shoulders as she prayed. It seemed a heavy burden had been lifted from her shoulders and left at that altar in our little Tennessee sanctuary. A scar began to heal that night. She stood up, face glowing, and slid back onto the piano stool and finished the song:

Take the dearest things to me, if that's how it must be,
*For I'm placing my whole life in Your hands . . .**

Sitting in my living room and recounting those moments with Cheralyn—that's when I knew it wasn't Michael we were waiting to hear about—it was Charlotta.

I went to the phone and dialed the department store in Nashville where Charlotta was supposed to be answering the phone. Charlotta's coworkers were puzzled and concerned. Sis hadn't showed up at work that morning. No call, no word. That wasn't like Charlotta. I called Paul Wayne. I told him what I knew, and he said, "Oh, my goodness—I'm gonna get that girl. Bless her heart. I'll bet she's a nervous wreck about messing up her car." He said he'd make a few calls and find out where Mom and Dad were picking her up.

I had barely laid the phone down when it rang again. I will never forget the sound of my father's voice. It was so broken and strained. He could barely speak my name. "Chonda," he said, "terrible news." And then he began to weep.

All I said was, "I know, Daddy. I know." Tears began to stream down my face, but I couldn't feel them. I was com-

*"Whatever It Takes" by Lanny and Marietta Wolfe. © 1975 Lanny Wolfe Music/ASCAP.
All rights reserved. Administered by Integrated Copyright Group, Inc. Used by permission.

pletely numb. Cheralyn slipped the phone out of my hand. I heard her ask Daddy several times, "What is it, Daddy? What is it?" She stood motionless while he told her. She began to shake uncontrollably. She threw the phone across the room and began to scream: "No, God—please! No!"

I tried to grab her, but she pulled away. She ran through the house. She crashed into the walls. She scratched her face and begged and screamed, "I want my sissy! Please! Please, Chonda, please get me my sissy!"

She threw the phone across the room and began to scream: "No, God—please! No!"

She ran uncontrollably out the front door and into the driveway. The mailman had just pulled up to our mailbox. Cheralyn grabbed his arms and begged him to find Charlotta. I remember mumbling, "Can you help me?" as I tried to pull Cheralyn away. This kind postman we hardly knew helped carry her inside the house. She and I sat on the couch, huddled together for what seemed like hours. Charlotta was gone.

On July 3, 1976, at 7:54 A.M., Charlotta Kay Courtney's car hydroplaned into the path of an oncoming vehicle and was struck on the driver's side. She was pronounced dead at the scene, the first victim of the 4th of July weekend traffic in the state of Tennessee.

The house began to fill with church members and neighbors. People brought food—lots of food. Sister Boyd ran the vacuum. The phone wouldn't stop ringing. Flowers arrived. Paul Wayne sat on the floor in Charlotta's room; he was in shock. Our family doctor came by and gave him a shot. The youth choir gathered in the backyard. Dad stayed in his room most of the time. Mother stayed busy calling family in South Carolina and Kentucky. Once in a while she would stop and stand in the front doorway and peer down the street. I just sat on the couch and stared out the window. Waiting. And waiting.

Finally a tall, frail body began to make its way down the sidewalk of our now crowded street. He was unshaven and carrying a backpack. A highway patrolman had found him camping in a wooded area in east Tennessee. My brother, Mike, stood at the end of the drive and dropped to his knees. Mother ran to meet him, and he buried his head in her chest and sobbed.

I had fought hard all day not to fall apart. I was waiting for Mike, my knight in shining armor. I just knew when he got home everything would be all right. He would wake me up and tell me this was just a terrible dream. He made his way through the group of mourners gathered in our living room. I could feel his hands around my shoulders. And if I could feel his hands around my shoulders, then I was awake. *This was real.* Charlotta was dead.

Every pew in our church was filled at Charlotta's funeral. People lined the aisles. There were chairs in the foyer and in the nursery so people could hear the service, even though they could not get into the sanctuary. The college president spoke. The youth choir sang, dressed in their red, white, and blue outfits Charlotta had helped design. A trio from the college sang.

◆

**We sat on the second row, piano side,
broken and battered, enduring the storm.**

◆

We sat on the second row, piano side, broken and battered, enduring the storm. The minutes drifted into hours that drifted into days that drifted into months. We simply hung on to all we knew—the second row. Sometimes we handled our grief well; sometimes we fell apart. Sometimes we were better, stronger; sometimes we were bitter and angry.

Mike took Cheralyn and me back to South Carolina for

a long visit. It was good to see familiar faces. Church families. Youth camp. Places where Charlotta's memory was so near and so real. It seemed as if she was still alive.

Slowly, one by one, and in our own ways, we began the climb back to our feet. Mother had her hands full. Our faithful "brick mason" worked frantically to strengthen the walls, adding fresh mortar here and there to reinforce the shaken foundation. She worried about Mike's attitude, Dad's depression, Cheralyn's silence, and my mouth. But she would not allow us to cave in.

Cheralyn's personality caused her to grieve quietly. Her silent and private pain was usually interrupted by my loud and boisterous objections to "God's will" for our lives. I tried providing a little comic relief. But usually the louder I got or the funnier I tried to be, the greater the evidence of my pain. The result? Sarcasm. Anger.

Paul Wayne went to England and enrolled in college there. Michael came home and filled in for Dad as he struggled with his depression. Mother went back to work. Cheralyn and I went back to school. Life on the second row, piano side, could never be the same. We could not imagine life being any worse. How could it be?

TO CHONDA

You're beautiful, little sister,
Your eyes so big and blue
Sparkle as you tell the world
How Jesus makes life new!
If only you knew what lay in store
For your future, talents and life;
You'd laugh at these "few" feelings
That bring you so much strife.
Don't feel you're less a woman
Because you're small and thin.
Love doesn't care for outward looks,
But what lies deep within.

You're growing up, dear sister;
I've been in your shoes before.
So when life's pains seem to get you down,
you're welcome at my heart's door!

With Love,

Sis

(Written by Charlotta for my birthday,
March 4, 1976)

DEATH

Death is all around
Black is the night . . . I fear.
Night is coming soon.
Darker it seems to get . . . I flinch.
Morning, dusk, and dawn.
Half alive they seem . . . I gaze.
Brighter comes the sun.
Radiant it glows . . . I smile.
Children arise and play.
Running so freely by . . . I laugh.
People walk the streets.
Sharing their hellos . . . I hope.
Strangers pass me by.
One stops, joining me . . . I love.
Life comes once again
Joy now fills my heart . . . I live.
(Written by Charlotta February 1976)

CHARLOTTA KAY COURTNEY
May 10, 1956—July 3, 1976

Technical Difficulties
on the "700 Club"

I HAD WATCHED PAT ROBERTSON AND THE "700 CLUB" for many years. When the invitation came to appear on the morning talk show, I was thrilled. Unfortunately, my husband, David, would be out of town and unable to come along.

I frequently travel alone, but it does disappoint me from time to time when I show up at a beautiful place that would have made a perfect romantic getaway for the two of us. The Founders' Inn is an exquisite hotel with five-star restaurants, a dinner theater, and beautifully manicured grounds. I called home the minute I checked in and told David, "This is the perfect place for a romantic weekend or a family vacation. It is fabulous!"

After chatting with him for a while, he reminded me that he would be taking a blank videotape to my mother's house before he left town. She would record the broadcast so we could watch it together the next day. As I hung up the phone, reality sank in. My mother? Operate the VCR all by herself? It would never happen!

I made my way to the studio the next morning and had the opportunity to meet Ben Kinchlow and Terry Meeuwsen. We chatted about what I would be doing on the "700 Club." The producer took me to the chapel, where their usual tour always begins with a devotion with the audience. I have never experienced such professionalism coupled with such spiritual-mindfulness as I did at CBN. I walked through the corridors with a keen sense that God's people were diligently working to further His message.

I visited the mail room and saw several of the studios used by The Family Channel. I also had the opportunity to go to the employees' midday chapel service, where secretaries, janitors, mail clerks, executives, bellhops, and others all stop in the middle of their day to pray, read the Bible, and have a guest speaker bring a short devotion to encourage them as they strive to make a difference.

I waited in the green room until it was time for me. I had about seven minutes of stand-up comedy to do as well as a word of testimony to share before the commercial break. Then I would move to the couch and have about a four-minute interview on camera with Terry.

As I stepped into the lighted circle and faced the small, intimate studio audience, I remembered Mother—she was probably sitting at home, panicked, with a VCR manual in one hand and the remote control in the other. So as the camera light came on and the producer signaled me to begin, I looked directly into the camera and said, "Hi! I'm Chonda. I grew up on the second row, piano side—and, Mother, push the red button on the front of your VCR now!"

After about 23 verses of "Just As I Am," my dad said, "Will everyone please leave your hearts and bring your seats to the Lord?"

6

A Broken Vessel— Who Ministers to the Minister?

WE WERE THE ENVY OF EVERY KID IN TOWN. MY father built playhouses, fixed our bikes, and taught us how to tie a hook onto a line and how to clean the fish after we caught them. We went camping. We sang together. He taught me how to drive a standard shift and to change the oil in the car, and the difference between the radiator cap and the distributor cap. I could change the points and plugs and rotate the tires by the time I was 15. I learned the names of all the tools so when he asked for an Allen wrench, I didn't hand him a pair of needle-nose pliers instead.

He was my daddy.

He also built churches. People loved his personality. He preached great sermons. He changed lives and influenced hundreds of people. He would take a church with an average attendance of about 25, and before he would leave, the sanctuary would have been remodeled, the youth choir would have taken several trips, and attendance would have increased threefold. He was good at his job.

He was my pastor.

Yet as far back as I can remember, I have always sensed a great conflict in my father's life. I was a teenager when I first heard the term *manic depressive* as I witnessed the effects on my father. These episodes would usually last a few weeks and would be as frequent as every six months or as infrequent as perhaps two or three years.

**My daily prayer is that someday
he finds sweet peace for what troubles
him deep within.**

I have had lengthy discussions with Christian counselors and psychologists as well as with my family about instances in my father's past, perhaps his childhood, that may have contributed to his ongoing struggle. I have had long talks with people who were around him during his most severe bouts of depression. I have explored with several therapists in my own attempt to understand my father better. But I am convinced that the worst enemy of his mind was Satan and his poison. My daily prayer is that someday he finds sweet peace for what troubles him deep within.

I was eight years old the first time I sensed something was not right at home. At this time we lived in a little town in Kentucky. Mother worked in the evenings at a hospital in the next town. My parents seemed to work very hard at keeping their marital problems behind closed doors and away from their children. Nevertheless, it was inevitable that their battles would spill out past their imaginary fortress, leaving wounded those far removed from the front line: the children.

A counselor once asked me to recall my most memorable childhood sound. It was "metal hangers sliding over a metal rod, muffled by the wall that separated my room from theirs." I can't count the times my father packed his clothes in the middle of the night just before his ranting and raving would turn into sobs of deep depression.

One night in particular Cheralyn and I lay in bed, listening to voices that weren't as far away as they sounded. Our bedroom door opened, and Dad stood there filling the doorway, his shoulders slumped and eyes swollen. I remember my heart racing; he barely looked familiar. His hair was a mess, and in one shaking hand he held a small revolver. I remember staring at the gun while he explained, almost casually, that he was tired. He had decided that tonight he would end it all and wanted us to know that he loved us and that he didn't want us to be scared when we heard the gun go off.

Mother stood in the doorway beside him, begging him to stop scaring us: "Don't put them through this—please." I remember her softly crying and trying to soothe him, like she did for me whenever I got a scraped knee on the playground. That night it worked. He quietly kissed us both good-bye and followed Mother out of the room. I saw before my very eyes the tower of strength that I had known to be my father crumble and be led away by the hand like a young child with his mother. *My* mother.

Cheralyn squeezed closer to my side. She cried herself to sleep. I lay awake for hours, waiting for the gun to go off. It never did. And it never did in all the nights following. But Cheralyn always cried herself to sleep, and I always fell asleep—waiting.

Unbelievably, our morning routines were hardly disturbed by those night encounters with Dad's depression. Most of the time he would sleep it off while Mother fixed breakfast and we were off to school. Out of respect for her weary, sleepless nights, we never mentioned what had happened. We considered ourselves unshakable partners in our secret second-row, piano-side society.

This was my world. This was my life. The secrets we kept hidden on the second row, piano side, remained just that—secrets. This was how we dealt with it. This was how we were *supposed* to deal with it.

Reflecting now, I see that we could have done things

differently. Someone could have gone for help. But when my parents were in trouble, there were no 800 numbers for pastors or their wives to call in their times of distress. Some churches now employ full-time counselors and therapists to help people recognize and confront the overwhelming struggles with addictions, dysfunctions, and depressions that plague many ministers. Dad could have gotten out of the pastorate and left the stress behind him. But most people expect pastors to be flawless, without blemish. We had seen men lose their credentials, their self-respect, their homes and families for a lot less than the troubles we were having in our home. The few times we tried to reach out to fellow pastors or their families, they seemed to quickly distance themselves and disappear. So we remained silent. The suffering would remain our secret.

My mother played the role of the perfect pastor's wife, mother, and homemaker. Somewhere along the way she realized that since she couldn't fix things, she would just try to survive. Besides, she had made a vow, "in sickness and in health." She worked overtime to see that our eyes remained on Jesus—not Dad, not nosy church ladies, not even on her—just Jesus.

For the most part we believed just as Mother had believed for years: that this rough spot in the road would be the last. *Seems like these times are coming less often. Maybe today when I get off the bus everything will be fine. Maybe Dad and I will go fishing today. Maybe he's dressed, happy, and singing around the house. Maybe he got rid of the gun. Maybe he and Mom are baking cookies, planting a garden, or talking about a family vacation. Maybe.*

Sometimes the *maybes* turned out good. Sometimes they were heart-wrenchingly bad. Regardless, life went on.

Besides, the church was growing. People were finding Jesus. Sunday School attendance was up. The youth group was going strong. Each church Dad moved to got bigger. Though the vessel was cracked and worn somewhat, it still held refreshingly sweet Living Water.

Keeping the secrets tucked away inside worked for a while. But as I got older, the conspiracy of silence frustrated me. The bitterness over the unanswered questions built up like plaque in my soul. I began to live with a level of inner anger that I never realized could exist. I began to blame the church. I blamed God. I blamed Dad. I blamed Mom. I blamed myself—especially myself.

**I blamed the church. I blamed God.
I blamed Dad. I blamed Mom. I even
blamed myself—especially myself.**

I thought that if I could just keep Dad laughing or in a good mood, then he'd be all right. No matter how much I tried to help him fix the car or paint the house, no matter how well we did in school, he still struggled. And I blamed myself because I couldn't fix it.

Several months after Charlotta's death, my father seemed to reach his lowest point ever. He was scheduled to go to a nearby college where several pastors were gathering for retreat and relaxation. After days of coaxing, Mother finally convinced him to go. It was only a 45-minute drive, and she urged him to find someone to talk to, someone who would pray with him. When I look back now, I see it was the first brave step they took to try to get some help. They were attempting to send out a red flare, to get someone's attention, to find another pastor to confide in.

Dad was gone for only a few hours when he returned to the front door. He sat on the front porch and put his head in his hands and began to sob. He told Mother that he had tried to corner a few of his colleagues, but instead of help or guidance, he sensed them pull away. "They didn't want to bother with me," he said. "They all gathered in foursomes and went golfing."

It's a difficult thing when someone so respected in the public eye stumbles and falls. It's even more difficult when that person is a pastor. Even worse is the reaction of the church. I have a friend who describes his aunt's fondness for gossip. He says she will listen intently, then deliberately interrupt with, "Oh, hush—now what?"

I have seen grace in action with some people. I know a pastor who let his guard down emotionally and spiritually. He confessed an extramarital affair to his supervisor. He and his wife entered a counseling program that not only restored their marriage but also restored him spiritually to the Kingdom. His supervisor wisely and lovingly cared, nurtured, and shepherded them back into the fold of the church without any public stone-throwing. He quietly moved him to another district, where his ministry flourished and his compassion for the lost and brokenhearted grew, and the Lord continues to use him to this day.

In a similar situation, another pastor found himself suddenly out of a job and a home. Without compassionate counsel he fell bitterly beneath his guilt. And what was once a beautifully effective ministry was gone.

My heart aches when things go awry in the church. Discipline, high standards, and rules are necessary. We all wish pastors were flawless. Think of the attendance drives we would have if pastors could be promoted as perfect! But I remember my sins, and I am reminded that within all of us there is the potential for greatness and failure. I am also reminded that we have a Heavenly Father who loves us even when we fail, teaches with compassion, and forgives without condemnation—no matter what our position is in the community.

As time went on and I matured, I began to realize that we weren't the only family who wasn't perfect. Our church and our church family were flawed as well. Since those painful days, I have also learned that my denomination doesn't have a monopoly on not being perfect. When you have a collective body of mere human beings, you will find imperfection. There are many scars collected on many different pews, in every denomination. I have also learned that we can focus on the unfairness, the politics, and the imperfection until we have forgotten the church's good qualities and, more important, its mission.

With a thankful heart, over the last several years I have seen incredible strides made within the Church, incredible changes for the better. Walls torn down. Counseling programs started. There are denominations working hard to salvage their fallen ones and restore them with confidence and compassion. Pastors are becoming more educated, more prepared. I applaud the Church for making tremendous efforts to remain biblically sound and equipped for the issues of this time, assuring the tired and broken that life in the stained-glass jungle can be victorious.

In our later years together, I held my mother in my arms while she confessed to me her deepest secrets and what she considered her most horrible mistakes. Her honest confessions made me proud of her. Breaking the silence and confessing openly the desperate needs of our humanness is the greatest affirmation of God's mercy in our lives. By allowing me to see her realness I have been able to forgive her silence. By being honest with me about her search for restoration, I have been able to follow her steps to the Cross. By openly apologizing to me for things she wished she could have done differently and seeking my forgiveness, she has exemplified to me the glorious redemption that should always be found in the Body of Christ.

On the days when the anger in my life resurfaces and I find myself wanting to blame someone for the junk of life, I blame Satan. He finds us when we're down, preys upon our weaknesses, and complicates our recovery with added doses of guilt and shame.

There was a clear cycle that seemed to plague my dad for most of my childhood, so clear it was almost predictable. Stress would begin to exhaust him. With the exhaustion would come depression. With the depression would come anger. Anger would lead to destructive behaviors and relationships, which would in turn lead to more intense struggles with guilt and shame. The guilt would drive his depression to manic status. This crisis would convince him and Mother that he needed prescribed medication. Or perhaps we'd move or take a trip—but we'd always get through it.

I was 17 years old when my father packed his suitcase for the last time. It was Mike's wedding day. Dad had been in depression for several months. Charlotta's death had triggered what seemed to be his roughest days yet. Not only was he battling with depression, but he also seemed vengeful and bitter. What were supposed to be the happiest times in Michael's life—the days leading up to his wedding—turned out to be very difficult. Michael became more of a father figure than a brother to Cheralyn and me. Sometimes he filled in at church when Dad couldn't preach.

Despite the circumstances, Michael asked Dad to perform the wedding ceremony. I thought maybe that was a good thing—*just act normal. Push him to the party.* But there was a dark cloud over my dad.

After Mike and Doris drove out of the church parking lot following the reception to begin their lives together, Dad put his suitcase into his car and left town. That night my mother sat at the kitchen table and cried. We held hands and she talked to me for the first time, not as her little girl, but as to someone desperately needing a friend. Her eyes were red and swollen. He had threatened to leave before. She knew this time he might not be back. She was too tired to beg him to stay and too broken to want him to. She looked at me that evening and asked, "Should I let him go or not? I just don't think I want him to come back this time. I'm really tired."

"If he comes back, I'm leaving," I told Mother that day. I was fed up with the whole ugly mess. I even told her to finish packing his suitcases for him.

"That proves it," I told my counselor years later. "It really was *my* fault. My parents' divorce is all *my* fault."

A few days after the wedding, Mike telephoned to see how we were doing. Mother told him Dad had left. He cut short his honeymoon and rushed home. He has always been there for me, always had the right things to say. I am certain that he has suffered a few wounds on the second row, piano side, as well. He has taught me by example what sweet, tender mercy is all about.

In the months following his departure, Dad telephoned once in a while. I am certain my personality and obvious bitterness made it difficult for him to communicate with me, so he talked the longest to Cheralyn. She always hung up with tears streaming down her face. But I never had much to say to Dad.

I felt abandoned and left alone to pick up the pieces of our shattered life on the second row: working two jobs, losing the house, watching the bills piling up. I was angry. I also felt that I was at fault somehow. My brief visits with Dad were disastrous—I was always the one to get slapped in the mouth because I talked too much. I was "carnal and rebellious—and would never amount to anything." I was the "middle child—the evil one." It seemed he never missed a chance to discredit anything I said or did. Before long I believed him.

To say that a great deal of damage had been wrought would be an understatement. As an adult who has studied the effects of dysfunction and mental illness, I can begin to understand why my personality began to take on some of the characteristics it did. I also understand that I can wait a lifetime for an apology or an explanation from my father, or I can let it go. I can allow the scars to paralyze me until I believe indeed that I'll never amount to anything, or I can be set free. I can believe that everything ugly in the world is somehow my fault, or I can admit that there are things in this world I cannot control or fix. I can spend my life trying to gain approval from my father and everyone else in the world, or I can concentrate on my relationship with my Heavenly Father, who loves me the way I am. I can grieve myself into depression over relationships that are broken, or I can carry my burden to the foot of the Cross and leave it there.

A few months after Dad left, a knock came on our door late one night. It was the local sheriff. He asked Mother to step outside. Cheralyn and I could hear their muffled voices. Through the window we watched the uniformed man hand her a piece of paper. A few moments later we found out that Dad had filed for divorce. The court date had been set. Mother held the papers in her hand. It was over.

I can grieve myself into depression over relationships that are broken, or I can carry my burden to the foot of the Cross and leave it there.

The second row, piano side, became strangely new—for the first time in my life it no longer housed the *pastor's* family. Now it was simply a haven for a few displaced laypersons. Our focus suddenly moved from trying to minister to the needs of the church to allowing the church to minister to *our* needs.

Families stopped by with groceries. Teens cut the grass. Men worked on Mother's tattered Ford. In the midst of our adversity, I began to see the church in a different light. It was not a show or just a place of employment—it was full of friends and encouragers. It was *family*—a group of loving, imperfect folks who have remained to this day—*family.*

I have learned so much by watching my father's life. I have the utmost respect for the man who raised me to the best of his ability and provided faithfully for me. But it has been difficult to maintain a relationship with him. And I know that breaking the silence of lifetime secrets will have its consequences.

I love my father. I can close my eyes and see the two of us, grease up to our elbows, giggling underneath the old Ford. I can see him baiting a hook or tickling Mother with a branch behind her neck, yelling, "Look out! Snake!" Those are the memories I *choose* to hold on to. That is the father I remember.

He will remain always in my thoughts and prayers. And I will keep believing in God's healing touch for his heart and mind. I believe that someday—if not on this earth, then in heaven—a father and daughter will walk hand in hand in peace, in honesty, and in the sweet presence of a merciful Savior who makes *all* things new.

Therefore, since we have been justified through faith, we have peace with God through our Lord Jesus Christ, through whom we have gained access by faith into this grace in which we now stand. And we rejoice in the hope of the glory of God. Not only so, but we also rejoice in our sufferings, because we know that suffering produces perseverance; perseverance, character; and character, hope. And hope does not disappoint us, because God has poured out his love into our hearts by the Holy Spirit, whom he has given us.

You see, at just the right time, when we were still powerless, Christ died for the ungodly. Very rarely will anyone die for a righteous man, though for a good man someone might possibly dare to die. But God demonstrates his own love for us in this: While we were still sinners, Christ died for us.

*Since we have now been justified by his blood, how much more shall we be saved from God's wrath through him! For if, when we were God's enemies, we were reconciled to him through the death of his Son, how much more, having been reconciled, shall we be saved through his life! Not only is this so, but we also rejoice in God through our Lord Jesus Christ, through whom we have now received **reconciliation*** (Rom. 5:1-11, emphasis added).

———————————◆———————————

All-day Singin' and Dinner on the Grounds

*S*HORTLY AFTER WE PULLED INTO THE GAITHER COMPLEX, *my sister-in-law, Doris, and I found ourselves hiding in the bathroom while more than 100 of gospel music's brightest stars and dearest legends congregated in the lobby waiting to enter the studio and record another video in Bill Gaither's phenomenal Homecoming Series.*

To say we were nervous would be an understatement. Doris kept saying things like, "Oh, the things you get me into!" as she applied a touch of powder to her nose.

I could only reply, "Why are we here anyway?"

Finally we noticed that the clamoring on the other side of the door had subsided, which meant one of two things: either the Second Coming had just occurred, or everyone had moved into the studio to begin taping. Since Doris was still standing beside me, I knew it must be the latter. We didn't want to leave the safe haven of the bathroom, but together we walked down the hall and stopped before a giant door marked Studio A.

Doris hugged my neck and told me she'd be waiting in the lobby, watching the TV monitors. She said, "Maybe he [Bill Gaither] will forget you're here and not call on us to do anything." That would be fine with me. After all, I counted it a great privilege just to stay in the bathroom.

The studio was brightly lit and buzzing with excitement. It was like the first day at youth camp. People were hugging one another and chuckling about old times, old stories, and sweet memories. And I noticed that no matter how old we get, the girls still scream and hug when they see each other, and the boys still clasp hands and pat each other on the back—really hard! It was a wonderful scene to behold.

A few newcomers, like me, sat with our eyes wide, watching people we had admired most of our lives. George Younce and J. D. Sumner were picking on each other, jesting about something that had happened at an appearance last summer. Jake Hess was grinning (Jake Hess is always grinning) and chatting with James Blackwood about a song that was popular when they were both young boys. Gloria Gaither was talking with LaBreeska Hemphill and Vestal Goodman about their outfits. (Those three ladies are beautiful in any outfit.) Mosie Lister was talking with some young songwriters in the corner while Mylon LeFevre, Eldridge Fox, and his son, Greg, discussed their golf scores. It was a family reunion, and I couldn't figure out how I had gotten an invitation.

Just as I spotted a chair with my name on the tag (even spelled right!) someone tapped me on the shoulder. I turned around and looked Bill Gaither right in the face. I couldn't swallow. Surely he was about to tell me my invitation had been sent by mistake! But instead, he said, "Glad you're here. C-c-c-can [Bill really does stutter!] you give me about seven or eight minutes, turn the corner, and sing a song?" I cleared my throat to speak, and he must have thought I said OK, because he said, "Fine. I'll call on you sometime in the next two days."

My heart pounded, my hands were sweating. For the next 24 hours I could hardly breathe, waiting and wondering! At least I wasn't alone—Doris had played "Jesus Is All the World to Me" for me the last five years. No sweat. When I told Doris the plan, she turned pale and said, "Now what key is it in?"

For the next two days I took every opportunity to fill an old hymnal of mine with autographs: J. D. Sumner, who signed, "God Bless You" (even his handwriting seems to have a deep resonance on the page); Jeff Gibson, who wrote "Ca-

naan Land"; Joel Hemphill; and Doug Oldham. These were my heroes. These were people who had sung at my church and had visited my town. I had their sheet music, their albums, even some of their eight-track tapes!

My favorite young female vocalist sat across the room: Candy Hemphill Christmas. When she sang "Master of the Wind" when I was a teenager, I felt comforted and inspired. When the Speer Family sang "The King Is Coming," I watched the rafters for the angels. When Joel Hemphill wrote "Consider the Lilies," I did. We had dedicated babies to their music. We had been touched by their lives and buried loved ones with the comforting lyrics of their songs. And here I was. It was unbelievable!

We had just finished singing an old Stamps-Baxter song when Bill Gaither looked across the room and said, "Chonda, come on up here." I took my place next to the piano and began to tell a few funny stories about growing up in a church. And I thanked them, with a grateful heart, for their continuing inspiration. Doris began to play (perfectly and in the right key), and I began to sing. When she hit the final chord of "Jesus Is All the World to Me," the room began to swell with shouts and applause. I began to cry. They stood and clapped. And the longer they clapped, the harder I cried. For a little girl from the second row, piano side, it was a moment that won't be forgotten.

Later, during a break in the crowded lobby, someone tapped me on the shoulder. I turned around and, once again, Mr. Gaither was standing there. He was smiling and simply said, "G-g-g-g-good job!"

> **And my little sister, Cheralyn, would always take up the offering—and keep it! She was very smart.**

———————◆———————

7

Cheralyn Ann—the Family Vet

THE YEAR WAS 1978, AND I WAS A SENIOR IN HIGH school, juggling two part-time jobs: I worked as a nurse's aide on the weekends on the 11 P.M.-to-7 A.M. shift and did some filing for my cousin's insurance business in town at other times. I also had the youth choir, Civitan Club, the all-school play, and weekend visitations with my father to keep me occupied.

"It was the best of times. It was the worst of times." (I hated English literature.) Our beloved second row was no longer comfortable. I was bitter. I was disillusioned. I was hurt. The very foundation of my family that I had watched my parents so painstakingly lay during my childhood had been shaken. Yet, at the same time, I had exciting dreams of college days, marriage, and career choices. Life for me seemed to be unraveling one day and then sweetly melting together the next. "It was the best of times. It was the worst of times."

Mother was working part-time as a secretary for the district attorney's office in Cheatham County. It was fortunate for her that W. B. Lockert was such a powerful man in the community, because Mom wasn't a very good secretary! She could barely type. But she was pretty good at filing. And she certainly needed the job. W. B. and his wife and children became our closest allies. After Charlotta's accident and Dad's sudden departure from town, they took us under their wing—partly because we needed friends and partly because Cheralyn had a crush on their son, Perry, and he had a crush on her.

We were learning how to cope with our parents' separation and getting used to words like "divorce," "joint custody," and "weekend visitation rights."

Mother was a licensed practical nurse at night at a local nursing home. Cheralyn and I were feeling like survivors. We could actually mention Charlotta's name without bursting into tears. We were learning how to cope with our parents' separation and getting used to words like "divorce," "joint custody," and "weekend visitation rights." We were beginning to feel alive again. We even found reasons to laugh again. And it felt good. Really good.

Visits with Dad were few and far between. I felt abandoned. We were working hard to make ends meet. I resented having to work so hard while at the same time trying to stay involved in school activities. But as soon as my sarcastic remarks would kick in, Mother would begin to quote scripture about children respecting their parents, and when that didn't work, she'd threaten to ground me—*for life!*

The all-school play made me happy. We were performing *Oklahoma!* It seemed to me the whole community was festive and talking like cowboys or farmers, thumbs in belt loops or pushing out the front of bib overalls. And every male wore a cowboy hat for weeks on end, whether he was in the play or not. It was the biggest production our high school had ever attempted. Cheralyn had the graceful ballet solo, and I had the leading role of Laurey.

Each performance had been a magical experience for

me. I had performed in many community theater plays previously. Mother took me to the local auditions for years, and it had been fun, but this particular time I fell head over heels in love with the theater. And the curtain call after each performance only reinforced the notion that I would major in dramatic arts once I got to college.

It was the final performance of *Oklahoma!* and Cheralyn had been feeling bad all day. Her fever began to climb so high that Mom insisted she stay home in bed. She was terribly disappointed to miss that Saturday night performance. She missed church the next morning as well, a sign that a visit to the doctor would be inevitable on Monday morning.

Our hometown doctor kindly wrote Cheralyn several prescriptions and urged us to see that she got plenty of rest and drank plenty of fluids. The flu was going around, and there had been several cases of mononucleosis at school. He expressed great concern that Cheralyn may have a very severe case of one or the other—and, at worse, both.

After a few days Cheralyn wasn't any better. She was weak. She didn't want to eat. And she still had a raging fever. The doctor had stopped by the house several times that week, and on Friday he made an appointment for Mother and me to take Cheralyn into Nashville to see a specialist. When we got to the doctor's office, I went to a pay phone and called Mike. He and Doris lived just on the other side of town, and he said he would come over and sit with us.

It didn't take the doctor long at all to draw some blood and to fill out some forms. He told Mother he wanted to admit Cheralyn into Baptist Hospital right away, and he called an ambulance to transport her across town. Cheralyn was frightened by all the activity. But after a few shots she simply drifted off to sleep. Alone, I drove the car into the parking lot of Baptist Hospital and began to get sick at my stomach. A cold sweat broke out across my forehead. I glanced in the mirror and noticed my lips were white and quivering. I wasn't sick. I wasn't crying. But I had that same nauseating numbness I had felt just 18 months earlier.

I made my way to the fifth floor and to Cheralyn's room. They had placed her in isolation. The nurse was being kind when she assured us that the reason for this was not to keep *us* from catching what *she* had but rather to keep *her* from catching what *we* had. I stood outside in the hall with Mother. Mike decided he should go and get Doris. The Lockerts drove up from Ashland City and insisted that I eat a sandwich with them. "Don't you get sick on us too!" I remember W. B. saying.

Mother agreed that that was a good idea. She was familiar with hospital procedures and knew that sometimes blood tests can take several hours. Cheralyn was still sleeping. We would not know what was wrong with her for a few hours.

There are familiar sounds and smells in your life that, by themselves are rather innocent. But in the light of one defining moment, even the ordinary can become chilling. For me the ever-present medicine smell of the hospital and the sight of a neat row of empty wheelchairs parked along the hallway turns me cold to this day.

As I stepped off the elevator, I could see my Mother at the end of the corridor, leaning into a doctor's shoulder, her face buried in her hands, trembling. Broken. The smells around me suddenly thickened. Everything moved in slow motion. My heart pounded in my ears and the roar of my own breathing was deafening. The wheelchairs lined up so neatly against the wall made eerie shadows on the floor.

As I walked closer to them, I could see the doctor's outstretched arm draped across my Mother's sunken shoulders, gently patting her back as if that was all the medicine he could offer her. *Wrongness* was everywhere.

Mother lifted her head as they ushered us both into an empty treatment room. I'm sure he had been kind and delicate with his explanation about what was going on with my little sister, about why she was so sick. But however kind the good doctor was, the words "lymphatic leukemia" came out cold and harsh and ruined any goodness there may have been.

I was enraged. I remember flinging my arms against a glass cupboard, the words "very little hope for survival" ringing in my ears. "No! No!" That's all I could say. Just no. *No, God, not Cheralyn—please. I need her. She needs me. We're survivors! Take me, God, take me! She's quiet and sweet. The world needs her, God. Please, God. I can't do this again!*

I remember the doctor asking Mother if he should give me a sedative. She just stroked my hair calmly and assured him that I'd have it all out in a minute. Mother was a tired and defeated woman. She pulled me into her arms. I sobbed. The next few moments seemed like a bad dream, and I was just sitting and watching it drift by. W. B. and Dot Lockert began to make the necessary phone calls to family and friends. It seemed like a matter of minutes before the lobby of the hospital began to fill with kids from school, with family, and with friends. I sat on the couch in a daze. Mike, Doris, Mother, and I took turns covering ourselves with hospital gowns and masks and stepping into the quiet room where Cheralyn lay very still. Within a few hours she drifted into unconsciousness, and her heart rate fell dangerously low.

---◆---

No, God, not Cheralyn—please. I need her. She needs me. We're survivors!

---◆---

I overheard Mother whisper to Mike that she'd better telephone my father. It was as if someone had splashed ice cold water in my face. I protested. I was angry at the world and especially angry at my dad. I was mad at Mother for calling him and mad at Michael for agreeing with her.

That night I don't remember where I laid my head to sleep. I don't remember falling to sleep or getting up. The hours blurred together and drifted past. The next day I found myself stepping off the elevator once again. This time the sight was a different picture, yet just as memorable.

The lobby was full of people who loved Cheralyn. Their love had drawn them to a small room on the fifth floor of Baptist Hospital, arms full of flowers and balloons and little gifts intended to help pass the time during a hospital stay and hearts filled with hopes and prayers. There were cousins from South Carolina, cheerleaders, teachers, school principals, pastors, David Pierce (he was like a brother to Cheralyn and *my* closest friend). There were *Oklahoma!* cast members, city officials, neighbors, and church family—*always* my church family—and Dad.

Twenty-four hours later Cheralyn was sitting up in bed asking for some Jell-O. That was a victory day! The school bused anyone with Type O+ blood to the Red Cross so that he or she could give blood. As Cheralyn got stronger, she became more and more curious about her condition. She was always very levelheaded and intelligent. She stopped believing in the tooth fairy long before I did. And when her cheerleader friends would leave her room in tears, she knew there was something pretty serious going on and began to demand an explanation.

On the third day of her hospital stay, the doctor sat down on the edge of her bed and began his all-too-familiar, kind explanation. Michael and I stood beside her bed as the doctor explained about white blood cells and red blood cells. Mother held Cheralyn's hand as he explained the importance of early detection, chemotherapy, and bone marrow transplants. Finally, the word *leukemia* passed through the doctor's lips. In a fragile voice, Cheralyn asked point blank, "Doctor, am I going to die?"

He said very honestly and seriously, "There is a chance that you will."

Her big brown eyes held on to huge tears until one finally trickled down her cheek. She sat silent for several minutes. Then she looked across the room toward Mother and said, "I'm OK, Mama. Really—I'm OK." She looked at Mike and me and bravely said, "Well, if I wake up with you in the morning, that's OK. But if I wake up with Sis, then that's OK too."

In the days to follow there was much talk about a bone marrow transplant. We all had our blood types tested. The doctors discovered that Michael was a perfect genetic match for Cheralyn. Although he was more than 10 years older, genetically they could be twins. Michael was more than anxiously willing. He seemed to float around the hospital with such confidence. He carried his Bible and his enthusiasm tucked under his arm. He was expecting a miracle and was thrilled to be a part of the cure. I think he looked at Cheralyn's entire illness as an instrument for miraculous healing, not only for her body, but for our parents and our entire family. However, the procedure could not take place until Cheralyn's body was strong enough to risk the operation.

Cheralyn's hospital stay was short compared to most cancer patients: 21 days. There were a few victory days. Just a few. On the fourth or fifth day they removed her from isolation, since the doses of chemotherapy were so large. She was a beautiful girl with a sweet spirit. The nurses were drawn to her and shed their share of tears each time they left her room.

———◆———

Even though Cheralyn was three years younger than I was, everyone knew *she* always took care of *me*.

———◆———

We would lie in bed for hours together. I had several occasions to tell her that I loved her. We giggled about boys. I apologized for reading her diary. She apologized for sneaking and reading mine back! We talked about school and what I was going to do when I graduated next month. I tried to get her to talk about what she was going to do when she graduated. She would just smile and pat my hand like Mother would do when she knew something I didn't. Even though Cheralyn was three years younger than I was, everyone knew *she* always took care of *me*, especially with Sis gone. Cheralyn was the one who always told me which blouse to wear with my plaid pants, which colors matched the best, and never to wear *that* color of lipstick again. Most of the time we would lie in bed together and never say a word. She tried to be strong for her sweet age of 15.

But the victory days ran out, and the nightmare days began. She got progressively worse. The chemotherapy made her horribly sick. The pain was so severe that her morphine injections became more and more frequent, until she would hallucinate and mumble incoherently. She had open sores around her lips, all through her mouth, and down her throat. She began to lose her beautiful blond hair. Her fever climbed past 108 degrees, and we watched her body convulse as they placed her onto an ice mattress. She lost so much weight that her skin would tear across her bones. She began to bleed from her ears and nose. This cancerous nightmare bruised and twisted her little body until death seemed a welcomed relief. She would ask Mother to read the same scripture verses to her over and over again:

> That is why we never give up. Though our bodies are dying, our inner strength in the Lord is growing every day. These troubles and sufferings of ours are, after all, quite small and won't last very long. . . .
>
> For we know that when this tent we live in now is taken down—when we die and leave these bodies—we will have wonderful new bodies in heaven. . . . The joys to come will last forever *(2 Cor. 4:16-17; 5:1; 4:18, TLB).*

On the 20th day in the hospital I laid down beside Cheralyn—just holding her, wanting to stay as close to her as possible. Her chest heaved and rattled at every breath. She would drift in and out of consciousness. She would talk about her dog, Tippy, one minute and the elephants on the wall the next. We would wipe her forehead with a cool rag until the hallucinations were over. Finally she woke up and sat straight up in bed and looked Mother and me straight in the eye and said, "Do you see that?"

I said, "What is it, Cheralyn?"

She said, "It's home, Chonda." Mother began to stroke her hair. Cheralyn gently removed her hand and said very sweetly, "I'm going to go home now, Mother. I want to go home now." She lay back down and went back to sleep.

Tears began to spill down Mother's face, as if she had just heard a sad secret. She told us all to go home and get some rest. She wanted to stay with Cheralyn alone that night. We left Mother sitting with her Bible open on her lap while Cheralyn drifted deeper and deeper into sweet sleep.

I went home with Mike and Doris. We drove back to their apartment in silence. I tossed and turned all night. The sun had just begun to rise when the telephone rang. I could hear Michael mumbling softly, "OK, Mom. Don't worry—we'll be right there." I was off the couch and dressed even before he hung up the phone.

We made our way back to the hospital. As we stepped off the elevator I noticed Dad and his sister in the waiting room. Mother was standing against the two double doors outside the intensive care unit (ICU) where Cheralyn had been moved. Michael turned to Doris and me and instructed us to take down the cards and put the flowers and gifts into boxes—no frills allowed in the ICU. He took out a piece of paper and began to organize a sign-up sheet for visitation. Only two family members were permitted every four hours, and they were allowed to stay for only 10-minute intervals. I remember Mom putting her hand on Michael's and beginning to pat his wrist. Cheralyn had picked up the same touch from Mother.

Mother whispered to Mike: "Honey, I don't think it will be long." But it was as if he refused to hear her. He just kept writing. Suddenly the double doors opened and Cheralyn's doctor asked us to all step into a familiar treatment room. He and Mother had spent most of the night at Cheralyn's bedside.

"Did she ever regain consciousness?" Mother asked before he could say anything.

"Virginia, I don't think so," he answered. "She went quietly and gently. She was very peaceful most of the night. I pronounced her deceased at 7:10 A.M. I'm so sorry." Cheralyn Ann Courtney, my sister, my friend, was gone.

Something happened to me that day. I shut down. I locked my heart and tried to throw away the key. A large part of me died with Charlotta, and the remaining pieces were buried with Cheralyn. Oh, I lived and breathed. I went to work. I even managed to chuckle from time to time. But the deepest, joyful portion of what was usually me was hidden away for a long, long time.

At Forest Lawn Cemetery in Ashland City, two heart-shaped granite slabs stand upright on a Tennessee hillside. I visit there from time to time. It is a beautiful place—but it's not home. When I let myself, I can hear their voices echo in my mind. I hear their laughter and feel their arms linked to each of my elbows. We're skipping together across the field chasing the cows at my grandmother's house. We're perched on the piano stool together, dressed alike, and singing, "Step into the sunshine. Get out of the rain . . ."

As the years pass by, it becomes harder to remember some details of their touch and the smell of their hair when it brushed against my face in our crowded bunk beds. Sometimes I get frustrated trying desperately to picture how tall Cheralyn would be today and envision Charlotta's graceful fingers on the piano keys.

But there is one place that I will always be able to see them. From the days when our bare feet would dangle in midair to the many times Mother pinched our legs and whispered, "Sit up straight—stop passing notes to each other!" It is *our* seat. Our pew. Our home. The second row, piano side.

Interlude

◆

On Sale at Your Local Christian Bookstore

*I*T WAS AN EXCITING MONTH. *I had finally completed my first full-length comedy video and for weeks had been awaiting the news of its release. Earlier, David and I had sat across a big conference table with Mary Kraker and Norman Holland at Chapel Music Group and negotiated a recording lease and distribution agreement with them. I had tried to be so professional, but deep down inside I was jumping up and down like a little girl. Soon my videos, compact discs, and cassettes would be in hundreds of Christian bookstores across the country!*

I couldn't believe it! For years, I must admit, I've had this secret fantasy to be hanging out in a bookstore—perhaps looking for the latest Max Lucado book—when I'm approached by a stranger who studies first my face and then the cover of my latest video and says, "Hey—isn't this you?"

Finally the release date came. I knew they were out there. It was time to check them out. (Besides, the next Max Lucado book was out too. No harm in jetting down to the local bookstore!) I quickly discovered that I didn't make the front window, nor the rack by the cash register. I didn't even make the bargain bin! Exasperated, I finally asked the sales clerk, "Where am I?" She promptly led me to a section filled with books about psychology and left me alone.

A few days later I tried again, then again and again. Nothing. (Although I did catch up on all the Max Lucado books I was missing.) Finally, while I had several days to be home, I called my local bookstore and asked if they could check their computer to see if the project really existed. The young clerk said, "Yes, ma'am. And every time we get a few of them in, we sell them all out the same day. We have some now, but you'd better hurry. They're going quick." I couldn't believe it. Complete strangers were going into their local Christian bookstore to purchase a comedy tape of me—and not Mark Lowry!

I was so excited. My mother is going to be so proud of me, I thought. I decided to hop into my car and pick her up and take her to the bookstore and surprise her; maybe we'd even spot someone making a buy. When I got to Mom's, she was putting on her coat and scarf and was in a hurry to leave. "Oh, hi, Honey!" she greeted me. "I was just going to the mall. Want to go?" On her dining room table were about 14 Chonda Pierce videos. I asked her where she had gotten them and what she was doing with them. She said, "Honey, I've been going to the bookstore every few days and buying these for Christmas presents. The nice young man from the bookstore just called and said some more have just come in. Your Uncle Gerald will love one of these! And Cousin Brad and Nancy—come on. We have to hurry!" She ushered me out the door.

"Going fast," the man had said. "I'll sure be glad when they put them in the bargain bin, won't you?"

On the way to the mall she asked me what I was doing with all those Max Lucado books in the backseat.

"Christmas presents," I mumbled.

The first night I was away at college I was lying in bed, and I could smell my mama's biscuits—burning. So I jumped in the car and drove home—Mom just lived in the apartments next door. Somebody had to help her throw water on the biscuits.

8

Prayer 101

THE DAYS AND MONTHS BEGAN TO BLUR TOGETHER after Cheralyn's death. Frequent visits to the cemetery. Horribly quiet meals around our table. I hated mealtime. Our dining room table was so perfect for a family of six. But in a matter of 18 months, the table had grown too cold and huge for just Mom and me.

My parents' divorce became final in January 1978. To me life had become a giant Don't Break the Ice game. You know the game—you take a hammer and try to knock out square blocks of ice. But if you hit the wrong one, the whole surface caves in. The divorce of my parents seemed to be that wrong block of ice. Things were caving in.

We couldn't keep our house, even though Mother was working two jobs. By day she was a secretary for the district attorney's office, and at night she was a nurse at a health care center in town. On the weekends I joined her at the health-care center as a nurse's aide. I'm not certain if Mother got me on at the nursing home because we needed the money or because it was a perfect way to keep an eye on me. Probably a little bit of both.

The decision to sell the house became a very bitter topic for us. Mom was trying to be practical; I was just trying to hold on to something. Amazingly, a man named T. E. Jones, who owned the nursing home where we worked and a retirement center a few blocks away, heard about our dilemma and offered Mother and me an inexpensive apartment. Mom accepted. Even though it was only a one-bedroom apartment, Mother called it our *haven*. I called it rehab.

I will never forget the day we put a sign up in our front yard that read, "Moving Sale: Everything Must Go." And everything did. It all had to. Cheralyn's medical bills were extremely high. Even though there was a small insurance policy, as well as the occasional donation from a charity group (I told my mom someday I could be a poster child for MD—Multiple Disasters), we knew we had to simplify our lives. Family and friends kept telling us a fresh start would do us good. So, of course, Mother and I began making lemonade again!

I dressed up in a Raggedy Andy outfit, complete with white-painted face, red-circled cheeks, a red-button nose, and red yarn for hair. For hours I stood in the front yard directing cars into our department store yard. At the end of the day we had "simplified" our lives down to a box of sheets and towels, our old piano, a box of old photographs, one bed, one dresser, a few clothes, a couple of plants, and one black trunk that held the memories of two beautiful girls. We loaded the back of my uncle's pickup truck and drove into Nashville.

Mother and I became roommates in a one-bedroom apartment. This arrangement came with its own built-in problems: she couldn't send me to my room, and I couldn't find a single corner or space to call my own. We had gone from a two-story five-bedroom brick home with a huge backyard that held a breathtaking view of Tennessee's rolling hills and the Cumberland River to a 15-story high-rise apartment complex that housed people older than my grandmother. Nothing here was familiar—except the college campus across the street.

Trevecca Nazarene College. My brother had attended TNC, and so had my sister, four cousins, an aunt, and two uncles. So during my senior year of high school, I had made it my intention as well. However, I had graduated from high school only a few weeks after Cheralyn's funeral. Mother cried bitterly when she told me there was just no money for college. We had decided that I would continue to work at night and find something part-time during the day—then maybe next year I would have enough for tuition. Or perhaps by then Mother could get a loan at the bank without all of this hospital debt showing up on her record.

There were fewer lighter moments for Mother and me but more arguments. My bitterness and sarcasm didn't help her much. She became more and more depressed. She didn't eat. We simply existed. Mother constantly begged me to go to church with her. So to avoid a fight, I would occasionally slip into a church service. I'd sit down with her and think, *There—this should keep her happy,* and spend the next several minutes doodling on a church bulletin.

Once in a while my brother and his wife, Doris, asked me to travel to a nearby church to sing with them in a revival. Mike had taken a job as a youth pastor in Augusta, Georgia (a move I never really forgave him for). Mike was a great preacher. I never doodled much during those services. I simply sat in awe of how he was coping—knowing that I was not.

I used to think my brother missed all the "good" stuff. I was 13 years old when Mike moved out. He was back for an occasional spring break, maybe a few summers here and there. But for the most part, he appeared during times of crisis. He would fill in at the pulpit when Dad was having a "complicated" time. He'd stop in to work on Mom's Ford. Because of this role he played, I viewed Mike as my knight in shining armor.

From our bedroom window, I watched the flowers bloom across the street on the college campus. Trevecca has a small but beautiful campus. The wooden bridge that crosses the cascades that wend through the heart of the campus—a bridge where all the boys have carved the initials of their girlfriends—became a favorite place of mine. The campus was quiet and secluded during the summer days. I could stand on the bridge and hear the water trickle over the rocks and search for my initials. I had finally found a haven.

Sometimes I would get a note in the mail from certain South Carolina friends I had grown up and gone to youth camp with. About 12 of them would be making their way onto the college campus in the fall. I was disappointed and sad to think that I would not get to stroll across the campus with them, talking about classes, professors, and the basketball games.

Then one day I received a letter in the mail from the dean of financial aid for Trevecca Nazarene College. I sat down on the couch next to Mother in our little apartment and read it with Mom as tears ran down my face. The dean, Everett Holmes, explained in his letter that he had been contacted by a Gerald M. Whalen of Cynthiana, Kentucky. Mr. Whalen wanted to inform the school that I was to enroll at Trevecca Nazarene College in the fall and that the bill for tuition, books, and dormitory fees should be sent to his address.

I was speechless. Uncle Gerald was the kind of relative you could love deeply but never really get to know. We would see him once in a while during the summer when we were kids. Mother and Dad would always take us over to his house, lecturing us the entire drive from South Carolina to Kentucky not to dirty the furniture or touch anything and to be on our very best behavior. In our eyes, Uncle Gerald was Daddy Warbucks (with curly hair). He was Mom's only brother. He had attended Trevecca for one quarter before moving back to Kentucky and starting his own real estate and insurance business. He had four kids, just as Mother had: three girls and a boy. He was quiet and reserved—nothing like Mother. But all of his kids were alive, and he was grateful for that. And he reached out in the only way he knew how and helped me go to college.

It seemed it had been so long since anything good had happened in my life. I was so excited. I was scheduled to sing with my brother in South Carolina the week before school started. That meant I would have to drive back to Nashville all night in order to be there in time for the Scholastic Aptitude Test (SAT). That was the only test I remember ever being excited about.

I began to prepare for college. Mom and I got word out that I was going, and family members throughout the South began to send precious gifts: a set of towels, a set of twin sheets (I'd have my own bed again!), a suitcase—which I thought was funny, since the dorm was a block away from our apartment. College!

Mother had begun to go to a Christian support group called Compassionate Friends. I used to tease her and ask her how her AA meeting had gone when she came home at nights. She wanted me to go with her, but I was conveniently busy. Looking back, it was a great involvement for Mother. The group helped her through some very hard times. She missed the girls and tried very hard to act excited about my living in the dorm. But she didn't look forward to living completely alone for the first time in her entire life.

However, Mother was never alone for very long. The apartment was filled with teenagers just about every day. College students were drawn to Mom's kitchen—as college students are always drawn to someone's kitchen! My best friend, David Pierce, spent every Thursday with Mother. And the maintenance staff at the apartment complex would spend all their breaks and lunch hours (with sometimes a speed round of Uno) in our living room. It got so bad that when someone needed a repair in the apartment building, they telephoned us instead of the office.

Surprisingly, my brother decided to move back to Nashville and finish his degree at Trevecca. It was strange to be on the campus together, especially because he is more than seven years older than I—but it was great getting to know him again. I have always taken pride in being his little sister. And I loved it when the upperclassmen chatted with me and called me "Mike's sidekick!"

I enjoyed strolling down to the married students' apartments and talking to Doris. We were becoming more and more like sisters, which felt nice. Mike, Doris, and I traveled from time to time to area churches as "The Mike Courtney Trio."

Once in a while we would drive past the cemetery where Charlotta and Cheralyn are buried. The heart-shaped headstones were easy to spot at the crest of the hill, long before I could read the names. I heard a saying once that "Sorrow is the knife that carves a cup for joy in our hearts." Time did ease our pain, but the scars remained, and my heart seemed emptied of real, sincere joy.

It seemed that just when I thought I would grow up and grow out of my bitterness and my anger, something would happen to leave me disgusted with life. Satan does some rotten things within our fragile minds. And he uses all kinds of people and places as instruments of destruction.

We were scheduled to sing at a little church about an hour from the campus. We grabbed a snack, our Bibles, and our beat-up Peavy speakers and drove out to the country church. We pulled into the graveled parking lot, and as we enthusiastically began to unload the trunk of Mike's old car, the pastor and a couple of his board members met us at the back door. They told Michael that they had heard rumors about our parents and other things that led them to decide that we would not be allowed to sing in their church this weekend. Mike said our good-byes, and we drove back to the campus, hurt and shocked. A deafening silence filled the car.

◆

They had heard rumors about our parents and decided we could not sing in their church.

◆

Mile after mile we drove. Then faintly I could hear my brother begin to hum. And softly and slowly came the words: "Amazing grace! how sweet the sound / That saved a wretch like me! . . ." He was crying. I sang and cried too. And so did Doris. But I wondered to myself, *Were we that unworthy? Does God's grace go only a certain distance and then stop? Are we damaged goods—so worthless that even our beloved church family has shut us out?*

We never talked about that night very much after that. I know it weighed heavily on my brother's mind. The double standards we have for one another within the walls of the church are not only unfair but also unholy.

It wasn't long after this that my brother and his wife moved to Ohio. Well, maybe a fresh start would work for them.

Almost 10 years later the Mike Courtney Trio was singing at a huge function in the state of Florida. Thousands of people were in attendance, and there was a big crowd gathered around to shake our hands, and some even wanted an autograph. An old white-haired man stepped out of the crowd and pulled my brother aside. I didn't recognize him at first. He told Michael that many years ago we pulled into the parking lot of his church, and he had been pressured by some of his board members and had foolishly asked us to leave. He threw his arms around my brother's shoulders and said, "Please forgive me. Please forgive me."

Tears rolled down my brother's face just as they had that night on that dark country road. My brother patted him on the back and said, "Oh, don't you worry about that. We never gave it another thought." My brother is an incredible man who has taught me great lessons in forgiveness.

The romantic image of the college campus as viewed from my bedroom across the street soon wore off. There were good days, bad days, good grades, bad grades. ("It was the best of grades. It was the worst of grades.") It was hard for me to concentrate. I worked hard to drown out the hurts and pain that I should have embraced—or at least faced. I just thought I could make a joke, have a good cry, get my mind on something else, and I'd be all right. Most of the time it worked. Sometimes it didn't.

I tried to bury myself in college activities after our trip to the country. I worked part-time at the college switchboard and on the weekends at the nursing home. I even ran for vice president of the freshman class and won. People asked me how I was doing. Some waited for the answer; some just asked in passing and walked right on by. I was loud and obnoxious most of the time, never allowing people to get too close, yet always in the middle of a crowd. When I took Prayer 101 I sarcastically made comments like "Guess we've been doing it wrong! That's why He's not listening!"

I made some friends and a few enemies. When I look back, I can truly see the greatest miracle in my life: that the enemy did not get Chonda. I could have easily given in to alcohol or drugs. I could have just run away—run and run and run. Whatever kept me from slipping completely over the edge? My survival was not a lily-white climb to the throne room. I battled temptations and lost on many occasions. But even more intently than my own battle with sarcasm, bitterness, and depression, a spiritual battle was raging. And within the spirit world, hell's fury was confronted daily by the thin, frail voice of a faithful mother's prayers. When I had stopped praying for myself, when I had stopped seeking Him, when I had wanted just to run, there were still people sending the word to heaven in my stead. People were standing in the gap for me: my mother; a little lady named Aunt Doris, who never forgot me; a brother, even though he lived far away; and a few college students sitting in a class called Prayer 101.

I had my share of dates on Friday nights, a few on Saturday, some on Sunday, the occasional Monday night football game—nothing serious until I began to date a boy who was studying for the ministry at Trevecca. He was a friend from my childhood. I still went out with my high school crush, David Pierce, from time to time. He was always a patient fellow. But this guy at Trevecca was a comfortable link to something I knew a lot about: church.

We would talk about church growth and ministry interest as if we were planning for a permanent position at our denomination's international headquarters. He was always enthusiastic about his classes. We talked about the mission field and the great missionary stories we had heard growing up. We would slip over to the music hall, and I'd play the piano and we'd sing together.

Then one moonlit night he dropped the bombshell. That night he looked intently into my eyes and said, "You know, you would be the perfect preacher's wife—except we could never get married. I couldn't succeed in ministry with your parents being divorced and all."

Kaboom!

His words exploded all around me. Again I was speechless. It wasn't until later that I thought of all the bitter, sarcastic, and hurtful things I could have said. He walked me to the dorm, and we never went out again.

I lay in my bed so humiliated. I didn't talk about it to anyone. *Who could I tell?* I wondered. I couldn't talk to my mother about it. She already felt as if she wore a scarlet letter. I couldn't talk to Mike—he was too far away. What was this guy's problem? I was certainly worthy enough to go parking in his old jalopy but not worthy enough for the Church? I was probably not even worthy enough for God.

**I dabbled in the world,
and it dabbled right back at me.
I was slowly slipping out to sea—
and my mother knew it.**

A few weeks later I left Trevecca. I kept telling Mother that I'd go back after I'd saved some money. I got a job as a hotel desk clerk in Nashville. There was no talk about ministry there. I dabbled in the world, and it dabbled right back at me. I was slowly slipping out to sea—and my mother knew it. Our arguments became more intense. Words got harsh. I had moved from sarcasm to disrespect. Mother had never tolerated disrespect.

She wanted me to finish college. I just wanted to keep her quiet! So I enrolled at Austin Peay State University (APSU) in Clarksville, Tennessee. It was about 45 miles from Nashville. Close enough for her to pop in every now and then—she warned! And she exercised that right often.

At APSU I recaptured my interest in the theater and music. Majoring in speech, communications, and theater allowed me to perform in several plays, musicals, and one-act plays. I met some incredibly talented people, and once in a while someone would chisel away at my tough exterior and get to know the real me. Dr. Fillipo was my academic adviser and my friend. And I met Dr. Mabry, a music professor who spotted me in the hall one afternoon, pulled me into his office, shoved a page of sheet music in my face, and said, "Here. Sing this!" He played a few chords, and I belted out the chorus of "Stormy Weather." The next thing I knew, I was a member of the APSUlute Singers, who performed a cabaret show every quarter.

One night Dr. Mabry introduced me to Joe Jerles. He was a director at Opryland USA. Dr. Mabry suggested that I audition for Opryland. It paid well, and I would learn a tremendous amount about performing. So I auditioned that winter—and didn't get the job. They told me I was too thin ("skinny" was their word) and that I should try again next year.

My days in Clarksville were some of the most restless I have ever experienced. I made some horrible mistakes there. The curfew looked good on paper, the rules applied only to those who wanted to follow them, and there was no such thing as Prayer 101.

Most weekends I would go home. I'd spend the weekends with Mother, watching TV, playing Scrabble. And most weekends David was there. He had become a part of my family. I confided in him about everything. We had watched each other grow up. Many times he told me I still had some growing up to do. He was right.

One night after supper, as we were getting out the Scrabble board, David said he couldn't stay—he had a date.

"A what?" I said. "Who's the bimbo?"

He answered, "She's the sister of the jerk you went out with last night!"

David had been seeing someone else for several months. I was furious. Mother kept saying, "I don't know why you're so upset. He's been around for five years, waiting for you to notice. He deserves to find someone who will appreciate him."

I drove back to Clarksville, mad at the world. How dare he do this to me? I'd show him. So that summer I left Clarksville and moved to Kentucky to live with Uncle Gerald and sing with his son, Brad, in a country music band. Halfway through the summer, David showed up at the dinner club where we were playing. He was seated at the front table, holding a vase full of roses. The card read simply, "Let's go steady!"

I laughed and laughed. Steady—after all this time? He has always been levelheaded—"Let's-take-it-one-step-at-a-time Dave.

I went back to school in the fall to Austin Peay State University. The Mike Courtney Trio was back at it again. We knew how to sing in church. We needed the fellowship—and the money for school. This time I didn't live on campus. I lived with my cousins, Jerry and Ann Huff, about 20 miles from the campus. They had a wonderful old farmhouse, and there were six people at the dinner table. I had thought I didn't really need a daddy anymore until living with my cousin Jerry. I needed him.

David was finishing his senior year at Tennessee State University, where he majored in journalism, but he attended every play or production I was a part of. He encouraged me to work hard, to concentrate, and to give my audition to Opryland another shot. We acted like high school sweethearts again. I loved the fact that he knew and remembered Cheralyn. She had been like a little sister to him. It was important that we had a history, one that was filled with more fun and happy memories than sad ones. He was a tranquillity base for me. He has always had a "mellowing" effect on me—something my mother adores about him!

I am blessed to have experienced several incidents where the Lord allowed me to witness firsthand His amazing restoring power. Moments of reconciliation. Moments of restoration. Moments of verification, when He whispers through these incidents, "See. I'm here. I see your pain. I know your hurt—now go and be healed."

One such incident occurred October 15, 1982. David was driving me home from a Friday "Cabaret" night at Austin Peay State University. He wanted to take a stroll in the cool night air at the farmhouse and enjoy the full moon. Suddenly he stopped beneath a giant oak tree, bent down on one knee, and asked me to marry him.

I said, "Yes."

———————◆———————

We were married May 14, 1983, on the front porch of the farmhouse that still feels like home.

———————◆———————

Then he suggested we kneel together and pray to God for His blessings on our lives together. The words he prayed amazed me—he thanked God for *me*. He thanked Him for keeping me safe and creating *me* for him. He asked God to "make him worthy of such a treasure as Chonda." I cried.

Of all the decisions I have made in my life, good and bad, the decision to marry David Pierce was beyond a doubt one of the best things I've ever done. We were married May 14, 1983, on the front porch of the old farmhouse that still feels like home.

Interlude

The *Herald,* Headquarters, and Other Terrifying Places

I'LL BE THE FIRST TO ADMIT *that when the invitation came to fly to Tan-tara (a vacation resort in Missouri) and speak before the general superintendents, their wives, the International Headquarters directors, and other important leaders of my denomination, I was nervous.*

I've always had an image of somber old men seated around a conference table with gavel in hand, policing everything I said and did. (Probably because every picture I'd ever seen of the general superintendents was of them somberly seated around a conference table with gavel in hand.) It was a wonderful opportunity that gave me ulcers. Afterward, I had an article published in the Herald of Holiness *(my denomination's monthly publication). I told my mother, "Well, I've finally made it into every Nazarene bathroom in the United States!" Because as far as I knew, that's where most folks kept their copies of the* Herald!

The small involvement I've had during general assembly, district events, Nazarene Youth Conference, and camp meetings has all been an affirmation to me that my ministry means something to my church. But no event spoke to my heart like being involved in the 1995 PALCON (Pastors And Leaders Conference). Looking upon the faces of men and women who can read between the lines of my humor from the second row, piano side, and know that they have, and are feeling, the same joys and the same hurts as me was like coming home after many long semesters away.

On the first night of these week-long conferences, Pastor Steve Green, from Pasadena (California) First Church of the Nazarene, would speak of the denomination's role in nurturing its pastors, who in turn must nurture their flocks. With an eloquent retelling of the well-known story "The Emperor's New Clothes," he spoke particularly of one brave little kid who could not be fooled by his superiors nor intimidated by the false prestige of their positions. With good intentions, a clear vision, and a boldness unparalleled, the little kid— probably blond-haired and squeaky-voiced—announced to the king upon seeing his new clothes, "You're naked, sire!" (This kid is my hero.)

There are many good things happening every day in the church world. And then there are times when the decisions or actions of a few seem to leave the rest of us sadly shaking our heads. I recently read an article about Rev. Jimmy Allen. At one time he was the leader of the Southern Baptist Convention. In "Burden of a Secret: A Story of Truth and Mercy in the Face of AIDS," he tells of the pain and rejection he suffered at the hands of his church family. He states, "I'm sad because the family of faith is dysfunctional and needs serious change." Every denomination has had its moments of failure. We don't like to talk about them or publish them, and we don't always handle them correctly.

When you feel the church has really let you down, your options could be as follows. (1) Leave the church. Pull out. You certainly have the right. You probably even have a good reason. You might find a better place to worship. Chances are, you may run into human failure again someday, and after "church hopping" you could wind up where you started. (2) Do nothing. I mean absolutely nothing. Stop teaching Sunday School. Stop singing in the choir. Just plop down on your pew every Sunday and pout. You certainly have a reason. Careful, though. Your lack of outward battle doesn't mean there isn't an inward battle taking place, most likely one that Satan has already won! You're cold, indifferent, and your obedience to Christ and His kingdom is suffering. (3) Stay put and fight on.

Make some noise if need be. Write a letter or two. (I've written my share, and no one's scratched my name off the roll.) Pray harder. Keep your eyes on Jesus. Worship, learn, and nurture your relationship with our Father, the One who can inspire us to live Christlike at all times—even when we are hurt at church. James Dobson once said the definition of forgiveness is when we forfeit our right to hurt someone who has hurt us. That's a tough job, isn't it?

The headquarters of your denomination may always be a terrifying place to you. And we may never change a structure we perceive to be in dire need of change. Even nondenominational churches are struggling with church politics and issues like Acquired Immune Deficiency Syndrome (AIDS), homosexuality, racism, and homelessness.

But the Church, the real Church, is pressing on. It is found in a little congregation in the Smoky Mountains providing shoes for the poor and teaching Bible verses to Native American children, verses that will nurture them, sustain them years from now. The Church is found in a beautiful building in California that nurtures former alcoholics, feeds homeless families, and counsels AIDS victims. It is found in villages in foreign countries where people are hearing for the first time about a Savior who loves them and died for them. The Church is even found in music and comedy when people boldly speak out at a country fair or on TV about a loving God and His Bride—the Chosen, the redeemed, the Church.

I stepped into the room at Tan-tara. Surprisingly enough, no one held a gavel or had an expression as somber as I had anticipated. One of the general superintendents, William Greathouse, stuck out his hand and kindly introduced himself. Nina Gunter, director of the Nazarene World Mission Society, hugged my neck and whispered in my ear— "Go get 'em!" And after a brief introduction, I stood on one end of the dining room and proceeded to tell them all, in that peculiar, squeaky-voiced way of mine, just what I thought about their "new clothes"!

When I finally got the chance to meet the real Miss Minnie Pearl, Sarah Cannon, I stuck out my hand and said, "Blah blah blah blah blah . . ."

And she said, "Nice to meet you too."

9

Cousin Minnie Pearl

FOUR DAYS BEFORE MY WEDDING I GOT THE CALL from the Live Entertainment office at Opryland USA in Nashville. I was to start rehearsals the day after I got home from my honeymoon. To that office I was a name on a long list of young people needing a summer job. But I was needing a lot more than just a summer job. I was ready to begin healing. God knew that—I'm sure of it. He also knew just the right medicine.

He had so miraculously sent love and acceptance my way. David's love for me and willingness to accept me the way that I was gave me a tremendous amount of hope. I had many rough edges. I was still angry and sarcastic at times.

My wedding day was an emotional time. I'd had so little contact with my father over the past five years that I barely knew him. But he came to give away the bride. I wanted things to be comfortable for Mother. I grieved for Charlotta and Cheralyn. It was hard to think that they were missing this day in my life.

My cousin Mary Ruth made a beautiful arrangement of flowers with their pictures in the center, and we placed them on the platform right where I could see them during the entire ceremony. I like to think they were there and didn't miss a thing.

The rehearsals at Opryland were challenging to say the least. Several weeks into rehearsal time, Bob Whitaker spoke with many of the performers one night about their "marketability" as well-rounded entertainers. He told us we were all gifted and that if we want to honor the good Lord for giving us these gifts, we should do our best to take care of them and to work hard to perfect them. He said, for instance, if you want to be a well-rounded entertainer, don't be afraid to take a voice lesson or two, keep in shape, eat right, and take your dance classes and rehearsal times seriously.

That's when I started chuckling to myself. I thought, *I'm in trouble here.* (1) I failed Beginner Voice. (Actually it was at 8 A.M., and I didn't show up very often.) (2) The last time I exercised was in my 10th grade physical education class. (3) I love pizza, potato chips, and Little Debbie snack cakes. (4) I grew up a Nazarene preacher's daughter, and I've never even been to the prom—much less taken a dance class!

Amazingly, I didn't have to explain any of the above to the directors at the park. They could spot it after the first day! They are professionals, after all. Joe Jerles had spotted something else in me though. He said, "You've got it!" To this day, I'm not sure what "it" is. I guess that's showbiz talk. All I know is—by the way he said "it"—I was sure glad to have it and even happier that he had spotted it!

So, with "it" in mind, one evening at rehearsals, Mr. Jerles asked me to read the part of Minnie Pearl. Embarrassed to admit that I'd never heard of Minnie Pearl, I boldly stood and gave it my best shot. As I read the lines in the script, I began to laugh. The more I laughed, the more the cast began to laugh. I read some more, and we all laughed together. I thought those were some of the funniest stories I had ever heard.

A few days later I stopped at the Minnie Pearl Museum and began to peruse the walls of photographs and memorabilia. At the end of one small corridor a large screen played black-and-white footage of Cousin Minnie Pearl from Grinder's Switch, Tennessee. I was fascinated. There she was saying a few lines and laughing. And the more she laughed, the more the audience laughed. It sounded like music to me. Her timing was impeccable. Her quick wit was hilarious. She was so natural, so boisterous, yet feminine. She was a thin-faced lady with a flower-covered straw hat on her head and a price tag dangling rather ridiculously in front of her face—but to me she looked more beautiful than anything I had seen in a Miss America pageant.

Halfway through the summer season at Opryland, several of us discovered a little secret. After we'd clock out, we'd sneak across the back alley, past the laundry where vent pipes shot steam out across the pavement (creating an adventurous 007 atmosphere), past the wardrobe department, and around the curve to the top of the hill. From there we could see the building. And once in a while, if things weren't too busy backstage, the guard at the back door of the Grand Ole Opry would let a few of us sneak in. We would either have to sit at the highest point in that huge auditorium, out of the way of paying customers, or, if we were lucky, stand quietly in the wings of stage left, and watch some of the show.

I didn't care where I sat or stood. I just wanted a glimpse of Miss Minnie. She would stroll across the stage in her gingham dress, stand beside Roy Acuff, throw her head back, and say, "Howdee!" and 5,000 people would "Howdee!" back. Then she would begin to weave her magic, reflected in the faces of thousands, with a tale from Grinder's Switch. And every time that sweet chorus called laughter would come back to greet her. It was indeed medicine.

A seed was planted in my heart during my days at Opryland. I wanted desperately to dive into a performing career. I worked hard on my skills as an entertainer. I worked even harder on my attitude. Yet, no matter how hard I tried to drown it out, something was still not right on the inside. I could recite the words and the stories. I memorized pages of stories from Grinder's Switch. But something was missing. I could talk about my sisters without the tears flowing as easily. I had an occasional conversation with my dad that didn't leave me on edge like it had in the past. There were temptations of every kind around me. Regretfully, there were weak moments when I knew I was breaking my mother's heart and many times when David's patience with me was near an end. I was desperate to fill the void.

I had some remarkable days at Opryland. For almost five years I was in and out of those musical alleyways. I also had the grand opportunity to meet Sarah Cannon, the real Cousin Minnie Pearl. She commented favorably on my impersonation of her. She was always a great supporter of the young performers at Opryland. I had the chance to work in several shows where she made a special guest appearance. It was a thrill for me professionally and personally. She had the greatest stories about the old Opry days and meaningful anecdotes to inspire us all to work hard and to be at our best always. Many times she passed on to us the same advice someone had kindly given her years and years earlier: "Love 'em [the audience], and they'll love you back."

Incredibly, my mother very seldom missed a performance of mine. (She has always been my greatest fan!) Mother had struggled for several years to find her niche in church again. She had loved being a preacher's wife; now she had found a new way to use her many talents and skills. She'd befriended a young pastor who leaned on her for support and advice—Mother's specialties. She thought of Pastor Lane Loman as a son, and to this day he calls her "Mom."

Mother advised Pastor Lane to visit with David and me on several occasions. So one hot summer afternoon— during the afternoon show at Opryland—as I was belting out the chorus of "Stand By Your Man" in a sequined dress, I looked down to see Rev. Lane Loman on the front row. Talk about uncomfortable! While I was kicking up my heels and dancing across the stage, my mother had sent reinforcements to invite me to church!

I thought for sure Pastor Lane would hand me the Four Spiritual Laws, a recent copy of the church manual, and one of those "See U in Church!" business cards as soon as the show was over. He just patted me on the back and said, "Great show, Chonda! See ya later!" No lecture. No disgusted look. He didn't ground me, and he certainly didn't forget me. He became a gentle friend. He was patient and understanding, yet firmly consistent!

Some pastors call them "the fringe." Some refer to them as "Easter Sunday churchgoers," "Sunday morning Christians," or "those just slipping through the cracks." I think Jesus referred to them as "lukewarm." Whatever the term, it is an unpleasant place to be, to say the least. You are outside looking in. You want to dive in, but something holds you back—anger, perhaps; aggravation. "My job keeps me too busy," "I don't have anything to offer," "You don't understand," "I've been hurt"—excuse after excuse after excuse. Meanwhile, relationships crumble. Children are born without any spiritual foundation. You become numb, joyless, and you can't figure out why you're not happy. Pastor Lane knew I had heard all the lectures and read all the rules. He knew that I simply needed a Shepherd, a Friend.

---◆---

She boldly talked about her faith, her church, and her love for God.

---◆---

One afternoon I read an article written about Sarah Cannon. It told about her talents and abilities to make the world laugh. It also told about her battle with breast cancer. She boldly talked about her faith, her church, and her love for God. She quoted scripture verses and talked about how laughter comes from deep within and is a beautiful medicine given to us by a loving God. I knew it was *His* medicine I needed and, more important, *His* restoration and salvation that was missing in my life.

I have certainly experienced a variety of emotions through the years. I have grieved, and I have laughed. I have been filled with rage, and I have felt the soothing peace of contentment. And for me there is no feeling worse than that of being utterly lost—from the very foundation that can anchor a soul for survival in life's most difficult storms.

Interlude

It All Began with SAM

*I*F I WOULD MAKE A LIST OF THE MOST-ASKED QUESTIONS *as I travel across the country, at the top of the list would be "How did you get started in Christian comedy?" For the most part, my entire life has been a mystery to me! I truly believe my career could not have been orchestrated to be as quickly moving or as sweetly blessed as it has been, had it not been for God's powerful hand steering the way. But as far as I can recollect— it all began with SAM!*

Saint Simons Island, Georgia, is a small arrowhead-shaped piece of land just east of Brunswick. As a matter of fact, you have to drive over a toll bridge from Brunswick to the island. It was here that novelist Eugenia Price found a Southern, romantic setting that became more than just a backdrop for so many wonderful novels, but almost a character as well. (Even though she never mentions the thousands of biting gnats that buzz around your ears and nose and drive you crazy!) It was here that brothers John and Charles Wesley were led to construct a retreat where those desiring to seek out God and commit themselves wholly to Him would spend days and weeks, many of those hours in the small white chapel that still stands on the retreat grounds. It is here where giant, gnarled oak trees, whose branches are draped regally with Spanish moss, are almost considered sacred.

My brother, Mike, and his wife, Doris, were asked to present the musical program for the week-long Nazarene International Retreat of Golden Agers (NIROGA) in 1989, all a part of Senior Adult Ministries (SAM). Mike called me the week before to extend a sweet invitation to join them in this beautiful vacation spot: "Bring the family. Bring your sun-glasses—besides, we need to do some old Mike Courtney Trio songs. Doris and I won't have enough duets to last a whole week!" Finally, the real reason for his invitation. Just before he hung up, he said, "By the way, why don't you bring your Minnie Pearl dress, because there will be a fun time in the evenings after the church services. You can do some jokes—or whatever it is you do. Oh, and I meant to ask you earlier, did you forget to take the price tag off that hat or something?"

My Minnie dress? That thing took up a lot of room in my suitcase. Besides, I was a closet entertainer in a very con-servative house—I could get excommunicated! Nonetheless, I knew the Mike Courtney Trio was rusty—and who knows? A joke or two might save the show!

About two days into the conference I put my lunch tray down onto a cafeteria table and began to cut my daughter, Chera's, sandwich into triangles when a voice behind me boomed, "Well, God bless you, Chonda. We're really enjoying your music. Mind if we sit down?" The voice belonged to Sam Stearman, the one responsible for starting NIROGA. He is a tall man whose face glows with excitement with every moment of the week. He introduced me to his nephew, Tim. Tim was much younger and much shorter. And he had that look. You know that look—as if he were in charge of some-thing—but he didn't say what.

Somewhere in the course of the conversation, Brother Sam asked, "Well, Chonda, what do you do when you're back in Nashville?" He would *have to ask! I took a deep breath and mumbled a few words, "I, ah . . . er . . . imperson . . . ah . . . er . . . Minnie P . . . ah . . . never mind. Actually, I don't do much of anything!"*

Did I mention that Brother Sam has very good ears, as well as an uncanny ability to take bits and pieces of what people say and make entire sentences out of it? In a few mo-ments he had the entire program outlined for the evening's Fun Time for Seniors, starring yours truly, with special assis-

tance by Cousin Minnie Pearl! Oh, boy! He also wanted me to be sure to share a bit of testimony and sing a song or two.

Then Tim Stearman spoke up and said, "Oh, this is great! I was just looking for someone to speak at the Senior Adult Banquet for General Assembly" (an international gathering of Nazarenes). "Perhaps you could give your testimony during the Sunday School Convention as well." So that's *what he was in charge of!*

Wait until I get hold of my brother, I thought. I was certainly making myself wholly available to God. David and I were active at church. I had experienced God's sanctifying power in my life. I loved working with the young people. I helped with the church bulletin. I led the singing—but, my "day" job as a comedian was an entirely different thing. I never imagined the Lord would be interested in using that.

As quickly as Brother Sam had organized the show, he was gone. I went to my room, where David and I sat down and jotted down a list of 10 Minnie Pearl jokes that would barely get us to 15 minutes. Brother Sam needed about 45 minutes' worth! So I told David I could tell a couple of preacher's jokes I'd heard as a kid. He reminded me of a few stories I had shared with him about growing up in church. And before long we thought we had enough for 25 minutes!

That night, on an island off the coast of Georgia, I stepped out in front of about 500 senior adults and said, "Howdee! I'm just so proud to be here!" After I had exhausted everything I knew about Grinder's Switch, Tennessee, I slipped my straw hat off and explained to them that was all the funny stuff that I knew—except for this one time when I was in church . . .

"You see," I continued, "my mother always made us sit together. I think it was the right-hand side—or sometimes the left, I'm not sure—I do know it was always about the second pew or so. Well, to be exact, I grew up sitting on the second row, piano side . . ."

And they laughed.

My favorite piece of advice Mother gave me was "If the Lord had meant for you to have holes in your ears, He would have put them there."

———————————◆———————————

10

Homesick

DAVID AND I WERE SURPRISED EARLY IN OUR marriage with an incredible gift: a baby girl. I had a very difficult pregnancy. Chera Kay was almost 4 years old when we began to talk about a sibling, but it was so hard to imagine another pregnancy with the physical challenge and summer heat at Opryland. So in 1987 I left Opryland and found a desk job. I continued to impersonate Minnie Pearl for the Opryland Talent Agency at special events from time to time. It continued to be a much-needed medicine—a wonderful medicine.

I applied for a secretarial job on the famous Music Row in Nashville. A song publisher was in need of a receptionist. A friend of mine recommended me, and I started my new adventure. Several months later I found myself not only answering the phone, but also listening to the songs being written all around me. I had the opportunity to meet some incredible songwriters and some famous entertainers.

It seemed that on the surface our lives seemed to settle down. Mother had met a wonderful man at her church. I was so shocked when my brother telephoned to tell me that Samuel Farless had called him long-distance and asked if he could have Mike's permission to "take Mother out for lunch next Sunday." I guess I never thought about her getting married again. Evidently lunch went well— three months later she and "Papa Sam" were married. My daughter attached herself very quickly to Papa Sam, and he very quickly attached himself to her.

Mother and I rarely argued anymore. She nudged me from time to time to visit with her at church. I was trying to do all the right things. I went through a lot of the motions at least. But I was *empty*. In my search for fulfillment, I had found nothing—absolutely nothing—that the world offered that could fill the void in my life. No success, no achievements. No amount of status brought real peace. Not alcohol. Not drugs. Nothing. Nothing seemed to soothe the restlessness deep within my soul.

———◆———

**Could it be that the Holy Spirit
was moving like the breath of God
through this way, this day, this place?**

———◆———

One afternoon while sitting at my desk, I ran across a cassette tape that needed the routine attention I gave to items left on my desk. It was my job to listen to the tape, transcribe the lyrics, catalog the necessary writer information, fill out the copyright form, and make a few notes suggesting recording artist and producers who might be interested. I remembered this particular cassette, since my boss had introduced me to the writer the day before. She was a very pleasant lady named Linda. Oddly, the phone on my desk didn't ring a single time as I listened. (I rarely made it through the first verse of a song before I had to stop and answer the phone.) The other writers in the building were quietly content with the coffeepot, the copy machine didn't run out of paper, and my boss, Judy Harris, was occupied on the phone the entire length of the song. It was in this stillness that something happened.

The words began to penetrate my being, unexpectedly, like a breeze that takes your breath away on a beautiful fall day. I sat motionless, unable to type a word as they passed through the air by me, around me, and through me—like Mother's voice when I was a little girl, soothing the hurt, loving away the pain of a scraped knee. Could it be that the Holy Spirit was whisking through this way? On this day? In this place?

> *When life gets you down, and no matter who*
> *you're with you feel alone.*
> *You know there must be more to life than*
> *feeling like you're far away from home.*
> *And you've almost given up, on ever finding*
> *everlasting peace of mind.*
> *Well, believe me when I tell you, the love*
> *you're needing now's the Saving Kind.*
> *My life had filled with darkness, and no mat-*
> *ter where I turned there was no light.*
> *And in my desperation and loneliness I cried*
> *out in the night,*
> *"If there really is a God, if you're really out*
> *there somewhere, come tonight."*
> *As I fell to my knees I felt the power of the love*
> *I call the Saving Kind.**

I walked into Judy's office that afternoon and told her I needed to go home. She asked if I was feeling OK. I told her I just needed to go home. She asked when I'd be back, and I told her, "I don't think I *will* be back."

I stopped at the day care center and picked up Chera Kay early. She seemed particularly radiant on this day. We rolled down the windows in the car and drove to our little house on the outskirts of town. She chattered the entire way home. She counted the street signs. She talked about her day. She sang songs. She began to sing Sunday School choruses: "Jesus Loves Me" and "Only a Boy Named David."

*"The Saving Kind" by Linda A. Bolton. © 1990 BMG Songs, Inc./ASCAP. All rights reserved. Used by permission.

I looked across the car as the sunlight glowed across her face. Her face seemed so familiar. Oh, I knew it was Chera —I could hear her sweet voice. But another thin-faced, blond-headed little girl seemed to spring to my mind, merrily singing words she had learned in Sunday School and church—it was me.

———————◆———————

"You know there must be more to life than feeling like you're far away from home."

———————◆———————

For many years I had worked hard to pull away from all the things I had heard and learned as a child. A miraculous flood of memories began to penetrate my bitterness and my anger. The numbness began to leave, and I could feel every heartbeat, every sensation in my soul. Suddenly I felt such an urgency and responsibility for what was around me. The impact of parenting hit me for the first time. I stopped thinking about what had happened *to* me and noticed what was ahead *for* me. She must keep learning the words, I thought. She must memorize the scripture verses, listen to the stories, be so familiar with the sights and sounds of church—she must be prepared for life. And the only thing that could ever prepare her was a love that brings meaning to life, peace of mind, light in life's darkest moments.

The brightest light I've ever seen was shining.
The warmest breeze was passing through my heart.
The greatest peace I've ever known had filled me.
*For the Love of God can save you—no matter who or where you are.**

The same chorus that had flooded my heart while sitting in an office on Music Row swept across my mind again

*"The Saving Kind" by Linda A. Bolton. © 1990 BMG Songs, Inc./ASCAP. All rights reserved. Used by permission.

and again as we sat on the porch and waited for Daddy to get home. One line in particular continued to pierce through the numbness of my heart—*You know there must be more to life than feeling like you're far away from home.** No matter how much I tried to drown out the memories from my childhood, they were too powerful to forget. From the second row I had watched the faces of family and friends as the Holy Spirit would sweep through an unsuspecting congregation and jubilation would fill the room. As a young girl, I had experienced the incredible feeling of weightlessness as I stood from an altar of prayer with burdens lifted and sins forgiven. The scripture verses memorized in Bible quizzing, the choruses sung in children's church, the hymns from camp meeting, the messages, the moments all came back. All the experiences that had overwhelmed me as a child were now flooding through my adult heart. I was homesick.

I longed for a relationship with a King and Savior who forgives and forgets, who loves unconditionally, who brings peace and comfort in a troubled world, who opens His arms like a loving Father and welcomes His children home now and for all eternity. And I longed for all those memories and the genuineness of those same experiences to fill the hearts of *my* children.

I longed to have fellowship with a group of people who flock together lost, bruised, worn, and tired—who, in life's roughest moments, simply stand within His presence, following the Shepherd without the self-righteousness of thinking they know it all, but with the humility of knowing they'll "understand it better by and by."

Through many tears and long hours of Christian counseling, restoration finally began in my life. The Lord delivered me from the burden of responsibility I had placed upon myself as a little girl trying to keep Daddy in a good mood, as the teenage daughter who spat harsh words

*"The Saving Kind" by Linda A. Bolton. © 1990 BMG Songs, Inc./ASCAP. All rights reserved. Used by permission.

to her mother, who was working frantically to fix what was broken. I am grateful to pastors and counselors who had patience with my recovery process and kind words and honest prayers for my wounded heart. I found His forgiveness and His sanctifying power available to me, filling in the empty spaces and giving me hope for all eternity. I found sweet fellowship in His glorious Church and am convinced that the Church is the perfect place to raise my children. I may poke fun at its bloopers and hilarious blunders, but I am very serious about the role it plays in my life as a growing Christian. It is a *glorious* Church! It is a beautiful vehicle in which to learn about the Savior, in which to be nurtured and, more important, to fulfill the Great Commission spelled out in the New Testament: "Go ye into all the world . . ." (Mark 16:15, KJV).

It is amazing to think that a group of people, somewhat strangers, each with his or her own struggles and dysfunctions, find themselves huddled together—unified—on Sunday mornings, Sunday nights, Wednesday nights, during softball games, teen lock-ins, Bible studies, and women's fellowships. And the tie that binds? It is the Holy Spirit and the compelling love that drives us to want to be with Him, to worship Him, to know Him.

But whatever was to my profit I now consider loss for the sake of Christ. What is more, I consider everything a loss compared to the surpassing greatness of knowing Christ Jesus my Lord, for whose sake I have lost all things. I consider them rubbish, that I may gain Christ and be found in him, not having a righteousness of my own that comes from the law, but that which is through faith in Christ—the righteousness that comes from God and is by faith. I want to know Christ and the power of his resurrection and the fellowship of sharing in his sufferings, becoming like him in his death, and so, somehow, to attain to the resurrection from the dead (Phil. 3:7-11).

From the second row, piano side, I have been mesmerized by hundreds of sights and sounds that have molded my personality, my sense of humor, and perhaps my entire outlook on life. Some of the sights and sounds have been confusing, while others have been illuminatingly beautiful. One particular sight that I will never forget is the sight of my mother's face when I surprised her and slipped in beside her at church the following Sunday morning—into our pew.

I thank God for a mother who never stopped praying for me. And I thank God for allowing me to see my mother's face glowing, thrilled to see her daughter, her son-in-law, her granddaughter, her family reunited—at home—on the *second row, piano side.*

> *Train a child in the way he should go,*
> *and when he is old he will not turn from it.*
> (Prov. 22:6)

Postlude

George and Billy

I SLIPPED BEHIND THE PLATFORM from a back entrance. I was supposed to be the surprise guest of the evening. It was Fun Night at the annual training conference for about 200 people. I was shocked and amazed to be invited to such an event. I wondered how they got my name. (I must send a thank-you note to Bill Gaither.) My contact, Don Bailey, explained to me that among the attendees at this private gathering would be a few people in the audience, perhaps of some interest to me. He began to rattle off some names as I sat motionless in my chair—kind of numb. He told me not to let any of these names intimidate me. "They all need to laugh, and they are going to be so touched by your testimony. You will feel right at home."

As I found a chair and hid myself away and waited for my introduction, a kind gentleman stuck his head behind the curtain and said, "We're really looking forward to this. We're glad you're here." Though his hair was graying, his voice sounded so familiar. I knew immediately who it was.

I stood anxiously and said, "Thank you, Mr. Barrows. It is truly an honor to be here."

Before I could sit down, an older and deeper voice bellowed a warm and friendly "How are you?" I was hoping he would break into "How Great Thou Art." But he shook my hand instead, and I asked him to autograph my old hymnal. He signed it "God's Blessings, Chonda. George Beverly Shea."

Neither of them helped to calm me down any. If anything, my heart began to race faster at the thought of what I was about to do.

After a brief video presentation that recapped years and years of ministry moments for this elite group, I stepped onto the stage to share my stories from the second row, piano side. I tried very hard not to forget what I was doing. I wanted to stop and stare—soak it all in. But I went on with my story.

They all laughed and laughed—thank the Lord! Most everyone cried. But no one cried harder than I did. It was just too emotional for this little kid who had grown up in little churches across the South. And now after all the stories, the good times, and the not-so-good times, the Lord had allowed me to be here—here with him.

I had heard him preach. All of my life he has exemplified such integrity and consistency. The entire world calls on him when things go wrong. The entire world has been impacted by his relentless efforts to share the gospel message.

Why, I remember when he came to my town. I was in college and sat in the stadium with thousands and thousands of people. When the verses of "Just As I Am" rang out across the city, I went forward—four nights in a row—just to catch a closer glimpse of his face! It was the same face that was now in front of me, listening and laughing.

I thanked them all for inviting me and closed by singing a simple chorus from a simply grateful young girl— "Jesus loves me! this I know." I stepped off of the platform and walked toward an empty seat. Amid a loving applause, Mr. Bailey announced that someone would like to meet me in the back of the room. I made my way down the side aisle. Slowly and tenderly, this tall figure rose to his feet. Tears were streaming down his face as he opened his arms wide, and a little preacher's kid from the second row, piano side embraced one of the greatest preachers of all time: Billy Graham.

*　　*　　*　　*　　*

It has been an interesting process writing this book. I have never considered myself intelligent or profound. I have argued relentlessly with editor Wesley Tracy and my husband that I should not be writing a book. The few events I have shared with you have been very personally gratifying, but I never thought they would be of interest to anyone but *my mother. And as I peruse this manuscript, reading stories from my childhood, I am convinced that my entire life may be of little interest to you.*

I suppose if I had a clear picture of where I was going, then I would feel more comfortable writing about where I've been! I don't know what's ahead for me. I do know that I have had some grand opportunities in a very young ministry. I also know that I have a loving Heavenly Father who has fashioned my days far beyond any sculpting I could ever imagine. I know to listen to my heart when He gives me the opportunity to share with others the joy of my salvation and the love I have for His Church. Only God could have orchestrated such a symphony as the song He has placed in my life. So I simply rest in His care, knowing He will guide me along as I live within the holiness of His presence.

Also, I know I want to do my part to make a difference in the lives of preachers' kids across the country. We have a beautiful heritage as children of the call. I have worked these past several years to encourage other preachers' kids to celebrate their unique lives in the Church. Needless to say, for some of us who have accumulated some baggage through the years, we find it hard at times to function, much less celebrate.

I love the story of Lazarus being raised from the dead. I am not a theologian, but I do find it very interesting that Jesus Christ, in all His might and power, walked to that graveside, weeping with the family, grieving. And rather than calling 10,000 angels to remove the giant stone that lay across the entrance, rather than speaking to the wind so that the stone would crumble into thousands of pieces—He said very simply, "Take away the stone" (John 11:39). And they did.

So as it was for me, I want to urge you to "take away the stone" that stands between you and a true miracle of new life in Jesus. There are wonderful Christian counselors and agencies that can help you get beyond the baggage and the disappointments that have turned into a hardened wall or stone separating you from true peace and happiness. My hope is that healing begins for those who have been hurt in the Church, and my dream is that people stop getting hurt in the Church. I pray that your new life in Jesus will be joyously filled with the medicine of laughter—vibrantly productive—and that His sanctifying power will permeate your every pore until we can do nothing but celebrate!

And then just be ready. Be ready to tell your story—because you never know who may be listening.